IRON AGE HIEROGLYPHIC
LUWIAN INSCRIPTIONS

Society of Biblical Literature

Writings from the Ancient World

Theodore J. Lewis, General Editor

Associate Editors

Billie Jean Collins
Daniel Fleming
Martti Nissinen
William Schniedewind
Mark S. Smith
Emily Teeter
Terry Wilfong

Number 29
Iron Age Hieroglyphic Luwian Inscriptions

IRON AGE HIEROGLYPHIC LUWIAN INSCRIPTIONS

by
Annick Payne

Edited by
H. Craig Melchert

Society of Biblical Literature
Atlanta, Georgia

IRON AGE HIEROGLYPHIC
LUWIAN INSCRIPTIONS

Copyright 2012 by the Society of Biblical Literature

All rights reserved. No part of this work may be reproduced or transmitted in any form or by any means, electronic or mechanical, including photocopying and recording, or by means of any information storage or retrieval system, except as may be expressly permitted by the 1976 Copyright Act or in writing from the publisher. Requests for permission should be addressed in writing to the Rights and Permissions Office, Society of Biblical Literature, 825 Houston Mill Road, Atlanta, GA 30329 USA.

Library of Congress Cataloging-in-Publication Data

Payne, Annick.
  Iron age hieroglyphic Luwian inscriptions / by Annick Payne.
     p. cm. — (Society of biblical literature writings from the ancient world ; 29)
  Includes bibliographical references and index.
  ISBN 978-1-58983-269-5 (paper binding : alk. paper) — ISBN 978-1-58983-658-7 (electronic format)
  1. Luwian language 2. Inscriptions, Luwian. 3. Inscriptions, Hieroglyphic. 4. Anatolian languages. 5. Middle East—Languages. I. Title.
  P949.P39 2012
  491'.998—dc23
                        2012033894

Printed on acid-free, recycled paper conforming to ANSI/NISO Z39.48-1992 (R1997) and ISO 9706:1994 standards for paper permanence.

CONTENTS

List of Abbreviations	vii
Series Editor's Forword	ix
Acknowledgements	xi
Locations of Hieroglyphic Inscriptions	xii
1. Introduction	1
1.1. Discovering Hieroglyphic Luwian Inscriptions	1
1.2. Historical Background	2
1.2.1. The Hittite Empire: ca. 1680–1200 B.C.E.	2
1.2.2. The Neo-Hittite States: ca. 1200–700 B.C.E.	4
1.2.3. Cilicia	4
1.2.4. Karkamiš	5
1.2.5. Tell Ahmar	7
1.2.6. Maraş	7
1.2.7. Hama	8
1.2.8. Tabal	8
1.3. Biblical Hittites	9
1.4. The Hieroglyphic Script	10
1.5. Hieroglyphic Scholarship	12
1.6. Texts	14
1.7. Kingship: Religion and Power	14
2. Texts	17
2.1. Bilinguals	19
2.1.1. KARATEPE 1	20
2.1.2. ÇİNEKÖY	42
2.2. Funerary and Commemorative Inscriptions	45
2.2.1. TİLSEVET	45
2.2.2. KARKAMIŠ A1b	46
2.2.3. KARKAMIŠ A5b	47
2.2.4. MEHARDE, SHEIZAR	47
2.2.5. KULULU 4	50

	2.2.6.	MARAŞ 1	52
	2.2.7.	TOPADA	54
2.3. Building Inscriptions			59
	2.3.1.	RESTAN, QAL'AT EL MUDIQ, TALL ŠṬĪB, HINES	59
	2.3.2.	HAMA 1-3, 6-7	61
	2.3.3.	HAMA 4	64
	2.3.4.	KARKAMIŠ A11a	66
	2.3.5.	KARKAMIŠ A11b+c	68
	2.3.6.	KARKAMIŠ A4d	72
	2.3.7.	KARKAMIŠ A2+3	73
	2.3.8.	CEKKE	76
	2.3.9.	KARKAMIŠ A6	81
	2.3.10.	KARKAMIŠ A15b	84
	2.3.11.	KULULU 1	87
2.4. Dedicatory Inscriptions			88
	2.4.1.	BABYLON 2 and BABYLON 3	89
	2.4.2.	BABYLON 1	89
	2.4.3.	TELL AHMAR 6	91
	2.4.4.	ALEPPO 2	94
	2.4.5.	BOHÇA	96
	2.4.6.	SULTANHAN	98
2.5. Miscellanea			102
	2.5.1.	TELL AHMAR 1	102
	2.5.2.	KARABURUN	105
	2.5.3.	BULGARMADEN	107
	2.5.4.	ASSUR Letters	108

Text Publications	119
Bibliography	121

List of Abbreviations

Bibliographical

AfO	*Archiv für Orientforschung. Internationale Zeitschrift für die Wissenschaft vom Vorderen Orient*
Anatolica	*Anatolica, Annuaire international pour les civilisations de l'Asie anterieure, publie sous les auspices de l'institut historique et archeologique néerlandais a Istanbul, Leiden*
AnSt	*Anatolian Studies. Journal of the British Institute of Archaeology at Ankara*
AOAT	Alter Orient und Altes Testament. Neukirchen-Vluyn
AoF	*Altorientalische Forschungen*
BSL	*Bulletin du Musée de Beyrouth*
CAH	The Cambridge Ancient History
CHLI	*Corpus of Hieroglyphic Luwian Inscriptions*, Berlin: De Gruyter
DBH	Dresdner Beiträge zur Hethitologie, Dresden
Fs	*Festschrift*
Gs	*Gedenkschrift*
HdO	Handbuch der Orientalistik. Leiden: Brill
HS	see *KZ*
IncLing	*Incontri Linguistici*
JIES	*Journal of Indo-European Studies*
JRAS	*Journal of the Royal Asiatic Society of Great Britain and Ireland*
JSS	*Journal of Semitic Studies*
Kadmos	*Kadmos. Zeitschrift für vor- und frühgriechische Epigraphik*
Kratylos	*Kratylos. Kritisches Berichts- und Rezensionsorgan für indogermanische und allgemeine Sprachwissenschaft*
Kubaba	*Kubaba*

KZ	(Kuhns) Zeitschrift für vergleichende Sprachforschung 1–100 (1952–1987), renamed Historische Sprachforschung, abbr. HS (1988–)
MAOG	Mitteilungen der altorientalischen Gesellschaft
MSS	Münchner Studien zur Sprachwissenschaft
MVAG	Mitteilungen der vorderasiatischen Gesellschaft
MVAeG	Mitteilungen der vorderasiatisch-ägyptischen Gesellschaft
Or	Orientalia
Oriens	Oriens. Journal of the International Society for Oriental Research
RHA	Revue hittite et asianique. Paris
SAOC	Studies in Ancient Oriental Civilizations
SMEA	Studi micenei ed egeo-anatolico
Sprache	Die Sprache. Zeitschrift für Sprachwissenschaft
StBoT	Studien zu den Boğazköy-Texten
Syria	Syria, Revue d'art oriental et d'archéologie, publiée par l'Institut français d'archeologie du Proche-Orient, Beyrouth
THeth	Texte der Hethiter
TMO	Traveaux de la maison de l'orient et de la méditerranée. Lyon
WdO	Die Welt des Orients
WZKM	Wiener Zeitschrift für die Kunde des Morgenlandes

SIGNS AND SYMBOLS

*(numeral)	sign number after Laroche 1960
*(word)	reconstructed word or form
§	clause
⟨ ⟩	signs partially preserved
[ ]	signs not preserved
⟨…⟩	text damaged
[…]	text broken
[sign]	text restored (as required by context and/or attested in parallel inscriptions)
<…>	erroneous omission
<<…>>	erroneous inclusion
?	uncertain reading
?!	highly uncertain reading
!	amended reading
X, x	unidentified sign or trace thereof

Series Editor's Foreword

Writings from the Ancient World is designed to provide up-to-date, readable English translations of writings recovered from the ancient Near East.

The series is intended to serve the interests of general readers, students, and educators who wish to explore the ancient Near Eastern roots of Western civilization or to compare these earliest written expressions of human thought and activity with writings from other parts of the world. It should also be useful to scholars in the humanities or social sciences who need clear, reliable translations of ancient Near Eastern materials for comparative purposes. Specialists in particular areas of the ancient Near East who need access to texts in the scripts and languages of other areas will also find these translations helpful. Given the wide range of materials translated in the series, different volumes will appeal to different interests. However, these translations make available to all readers of English the world's earliest traditions as well as valuable sources of information on daily life, history, religion, and the like in the preclassical world.

The translators of the various volumes in this series are specialists in the particular languages and have based their work on the original sources and the most recent research. In their translations they attempt to convey as much as possible of the original texts in fluent, current English. In the introductions, notes, glossaries, maps, and chronological tables, they aim to provide the essential information for an appreciation of these ancient documents.

The ancient Near East reached from Egypt to Iran and, for the purposes of our volumes, ranged in time from the invention of writing (by 3000 B.C.E.) to the conquests of Alexander the Great (ca. 330 B.C.E.). The cultures represented within these limits include especially Egyptian, Sumerian, Babylonian, Assyrian, Hittite, Ugaritic, Aramean, Phoenician, and Israelite. It is hoped that Writings from the Ancient World will eventually produce translations from most of the many different genres attested in these cultures: letters (official and private), myths, diplomatic documents, hymns, law collections, monumental inscriptions, tales, and administrative records, to mention but a few.

Significant funding was made available by the Society of Biblical Literature for the preparation of this volume. In addition, those involved in preparing this volume have received financial and clerical assistance from their respective institutions. Were it not for these expressions of confidence in our work, the arduous tasks of preparation, translation, editing, and publication could not have been accomplished or even undertaken. It is the hope of all who have worked with the Writings from the Ancient World series that our translations will open up new horizons and deepen the humanity of all who read these volumes.

Theodore J. Lewis
The Johns Hopkins University

Acknowledgements

First and foremost, I would like to thank Prof. H. Craig Melchert who edited the volume. As always, he has been very generous with his help, answering my questions, offering advice, encouragement, and corrections. I have also benefitted from countless exchanges with Dr. Ilya Yakubovich and am indebted to Dr. Reinhard G. Lehmann for discussion of the Phoenician inscriptions. I would further like to thank Zsolt Simon, Shai Gordin, and Elifta Fritzsche for kindly supporting me on numerous occasions. I would also like to thank Marie-Odile Rousset for providing me with photos of the new TALL ŠṬĪB inscription. Any remaining inconsistencies and inaccuracies are my responsibility alone.

I would also like to thank the team at the Society of Biblical Literature for their part in making this book possible. Last but not least, I would like to thank my husband for supporting me in this endeavor.

Locations of Hieroglyphic Inscriptions

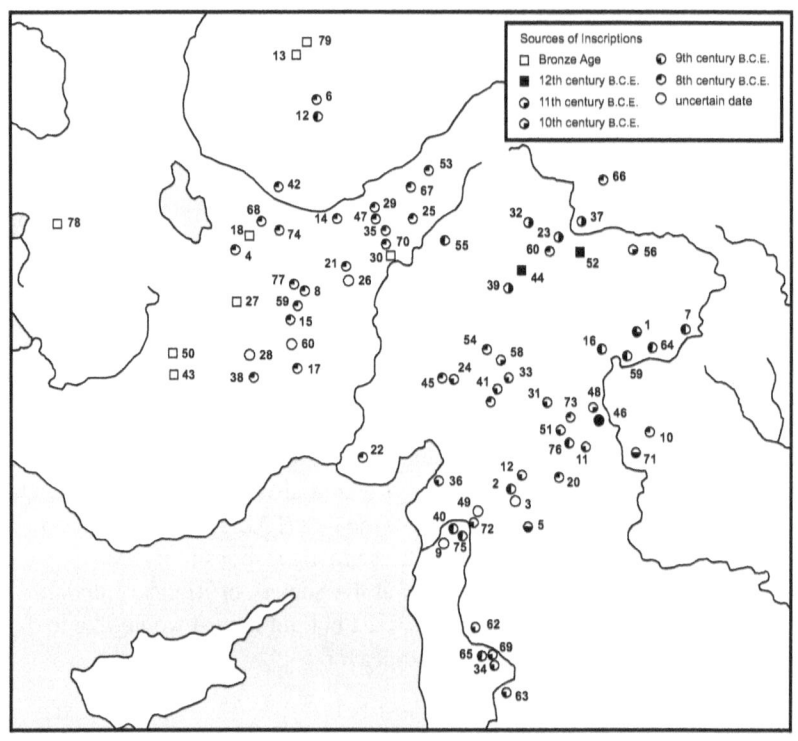

1. Adıyaman	21. Çiftlik	41. Karaburçlu	61. Porsuk
2. Afrin	22. Çineköy	42. Karaburun	62. Qal'at el Mudiq
3. Ain Dara	23. Darende	43. Karadağ	63. Restan
4. Aksaray	24. Domuztepe	44. Karahöyük	64. Samsat
5. Aleppo	25. Eğrek	45. Karatepe	65. Sheizar-Meharde
6. Alişar	26. Eğriköy	46. Karkamiš	66. Şırzı
7. Ancoz	27. Emirgazi	47. Kayseri	67. Sultanhan
8. Andaval	28. Ereğli	48. Kelekli	68. Suvasa
9. Antakya	29. Erkilet	49. Kırçoğlu	69. Tall Šṭīb
10. Arslantaş	30. Fraktin	50. Kızıldağ	70. Tekirderbent
11. Asmacık	31. Gaziantep	51. Körkün	71. Tell Ahmar
12. 'Azaz	32. Gürün	52. Kötükale	72. Tell Tayinat
13. Boğazköy	33. Hacibebekli	53. Kululu	73. Tilsevet
14. Bohça	34. Hama	54. Kürtül	74. Topada
15. Bor	35. Hisarcık	55. Kurubel	75. Tuleil
16. Boybeypınarı	36. İskenderun	56. Malatya	76. Tünp
17. Bulgarmaden	37. İspekçür	57. Malpınar	77. Veliisa
18. Burunkaya	38. İvriz	58. Maraş	78. Yalburt
19. Çalapverdi	39. Izgın	59. Niğde	79. Yazılıkaya
20. Cekke	40. Jisr el Hadid	60. Palanga	

Map used with permission of Harrassowitz Verlag.

1. Introduction

1.1. Discovering Hieroglyphic Luwian Inscriptions

In 1812, the first hieroglyphic Luwian inscriptions came to the notice of a modern-day traveller and orientalist, the Swiss Johann Ludwig Burckhardt—more than two and a half thousand years after they were executed. Burckhardt, travelling through Syria, recorded the following brief note about an inscribed stone he discovered in the city of Hama, biblical Hamath: "but in the corner of a house in the Bazar is a stone with a number of small figures and signs, which appears to be a kind of hieroglyphical writing, though it does not resemble that of Egypt."[1]

This description did not generate much interest at the time. Almost sixty years later, Richard Francis Burton noted:

> An important inquiry ... made me set out on February 22d for Hums (Emesa), and Hamáh (Hamath, Epiphaneia), on the northern borders of the consular district of Damascus. At the latter place ... I examined and sent home native facsimiles of the four unique basaltic stones, whose characters, raised in cameo, apparently represent a system of local hieroglyphics peculiar to this part of Syria, and form the connecting link between picture-writing and the true syllabarium.[2]

In 1870, Augustus Johnson and S. Jessup tried in vain to obtain copies of the stone mentioned by Burckhardt (Friedrich 1969: 128). In 1872, the Irish missionary William Wright kindled the Turkish governor's interest in this stone. With difficulty, Wright and Green took plaster casts, and a copy each was sent to the British Museum (Wright 1886: 1–12). The stones themselves (now known

---

1. "Journal of a Tour from Aleppo to Damascus, Through the Valley of the Orontes and Mount Libanus, in February and March, 1812," *Travels in Syria and the Holy Land* (London: Murray, 1822). Online: http://ebooks.adelaide.edu.au/b/burckhardt/john_lewis/syria/chapter3.html.

2. Richard Francis Burton and Charles F. Tyrwhitt-Drake, *Unexplored Syria* (2 vols.; London: Tinsley Bros., 1872). Online: http://burtoniana.org/books/1872-Unexplored%20Syria/unexploredsyria-ocr-vol1.htm.

as HAMA 1–4) were removed to İstanbul Museum in 1877. Similar stones came to light in various places in Syria during the 1870s, and among the first to attempt a decipherment was the British assyriologist A. H. Sayce. In a lecture to the Society of Biblical Archaeology, given on May 2, 1876, he proposed to use the term "Hittite" (from Old Testament *ḥtym*, Egyptian *ḫt'* or *Kheta*, Assyrian *Ḫatti*) for the growing corpus of hieroglyphic inscriptions. In 1879, Sayce connected the "Hittite" finds of Syria with similar remains discovered in Anatolia. In 1882, he announced that the Hittites were much more than the small Canaanite tribe mentioned in the Old Testament, namely, the people of "a lost Hittite Empire."

Almost fifty years earlier, in 1834, the French explorer Charles Texier stumbled across the ruins of what would prove to be the capital city of the Hittite Empire during his search for Tavium, an important Celtic city. Locals had directed him to the ruins of Boğazköy, some 150 km east of Ankara. Texier arrived to find the remains of a vast city, and outside of the city, about half an hour's walk away, an ancient rock sanctuary. It has two natural chambers decorated with figures of deities cut into the rock, their names inscribed in hieroglyphs. The very beginnings of this hieroglyphic script are still clouded in obscurity, but the first full length inscriptions were executed as official monuments of the Hittite Empire. While the discovery of hieroglyphic inscriptions in Syria predated modern knowledge of the Hittite Empire, decipherment only became possible through knowledge of the Hittite language, as documented on thousands of cuneiform-inscribed clay tablets. To establish the necessary background, we shall in the following briefly look at the history of the Hittite Empire—the historical and cultural context of the earliest hieroglyphic inscriptions—and of the ensuing Neo-Hittite States, where the hieroglyphic script became the only writing medium and experienced its golden age.

1.2. HISTORICAL BACKGROUND

1.2.1. THE HITTITE EMPIRE: CA. 1680–1200 B.C.E.

Hittite History is commonly divided into three longer periods, classified as Old Kingdom (ca. 1650–1420 B.C.E.), Middle Kingdom (ca. 1420–1344 B.C.E.) and New Kingdom (ca. 1344–1200 B.C.E.). All these dates are approximations, they rest on synchronisms and are based on the Egyptian low chronology. The following paragraphs aim to provide a short overview and will therefore only introduce the most important Hittite kings and events taking place under their reign.

The Hittite Old Kingdom starts with Hattusili I (ca. 1650–1620 B.C.E.), who rebuilt the city of Hattusa, a Hattian settlement that had been destroyed and cursed by Anitta of Kuššara around 1700 B.C.E. Hattusili made Hattusa his capital, and it is very likely that he named himself after the city. During his reign, he extended his territory to cover most of Anatolia and northern Syria. His grandson, Mursili I (ca. 1620–1590 B.C.E.) is best known for his military successes, taking much of northern Syria, including Aleppo, and even Babylon. This territorial gain, however, could not be effectively controlled or maintained. The campaign had drained the resources of the kingdom, and Mursili was assassinated soon after his return home. This introduced a period of chaos and internecine strife, until Telipinu (ca. 1525–1500 B.C.E.) stabilized the monarchy and formulated a legal framework for royal succession in his famous edict. His rule marks the end of the Old Kingdom, and the earliest hieroglyphic seal, the Išputahšu seal, also dates to this time. The Middle Kingdom begins with a period of which we know comparatively little under what appear to be weak kings. Tudhaliya I/II (whether there were two separate kings of this name remains a topic of scholarly dispute; ca. 1420–1400 B.C.E.) renewed vassal treaties with Kizzuwatna and regained control of Aleppo. He undertook many campaigns, among others against Išuwa in the northeast, and Aššuwa and Arzawa in the west. His reign is followed by another weak phase, culminating in the sack of Hattusa during the reign of Arnuwanda I (ca. 1370–1355).

The New Kingdom, also known as Empire period, starts with Suppiluliuma I (ca. 1344–1322) who ruled over Anatolia and northern Syria; control was exercised through vassal states and viceroys at Karkamiš and Tarhuntassa. Alongside Egypt, Hatti had become the main power of the ancient Near East, and this equality was acknowledged in a letter by a pharaoh's widow (possibly Tutankhamun's), asking Suppiluliuma to send her one of his sons to marry, as she refused to marry someone below her status. Such a marriage candidate was indeed sent to Egypt, but on his way there he was assassinated, thereby instigating a period of war between Egypt and Hatti.

Mursili II (ca. 1321–1295) campaigned in the west, in particular against Arzawa and Millawanda (Miletus). In ca. 1275 B.C.E., Muwatalli II (ca. 1295–1272) fought the Egyptian pharaoh Ramses II at Qadesh, in a dispute over Syrian territories. The battle is amply described in Egyptian sources as a resounding victory, but as the Hittites kept their control over the disputed areas, the outcome was more likely a stalemate; the gain, if any, was on the Hittite side. Muwatalli's reign is further important as the period from which we have the first datable hieroglyphic inscription, ALEPPO 1, a text of Talmi-Šarruma of Aleppo (see Hawkins 2000: 3; 19). Muwatalli's son, Urḫi-Teššub, acceded the throne as Mursili III (ca. 1272–1266) but was soon deposed by his uncle who ruled as Hattusili III (ca. 1266–1237). The latter concluded a peace treaty with Ramses II (ca. 1258 B.C.E.), a copy of which is famously on display at the United Nations headquarters in New York. Hattusili's usurpation introduced the final period of the Hittite Empire, which was accompanied by internal power struggles. His son, Tudhaliya

IV (ca. 1237–1209) still ruled as a relatively strong king—and executed quite a few hieroglyphic inscriptions—yet had to make allowances to Kuruntiya of Tarhuntassa, a vassal king and descendant of Muwatalli, who had a legitimate claim to the throne of Hattusa. Indeed, it seems likely that Tudhaliya's son, Suppiluliuma II, (ca. 1205–?) openly waged war on Tarhuntassa, after Kuruntiya tried to revolt.

1.2.2. THE NEO-HITTITE STATES: CA. 1200–700 B.C.E.

Around 1200 B.C.E., major upheaval and changes affected the ancient Mediterranean and Near Eastern worlds. The region formerly ruled by the Hittite Empire lost its central administration with the fall of the Empire. Reasons for this collapse are much debated, and it is likely that a combination of various factors contributed to it. There is evidence of large-scale migration, including burnt and abandoned cities. Bands of marauding Kaskaeans, attacks of the so-called Sea Peoples, famines, and war, especially with Tarhuntassa, would all have aided to destabilize the region, finally leading to the fall of the Hittite Empire. On former Hittite territory, several new, smaller states emerged. Culturally, they were significantly indebted to the Hittite Empire and are therefore known today as Neo-Hittite states. Some of these new states were already important centers of power under the Hittite Empire who seem to have survived the disruption around 1200 B.C.E. unscathed.

Hieroglyphic Luwian inscriptions survive from the following Neo-Hittite states: Cilicia, Karkamiš, Tell Ahmar, Maraş, Malatya, Commagene, Amuq, Aleppo, Hama, and Tabal. It is remarkable that despite coming from such a large area and over a period of almost five hundred years, the inscriptions are nonetheless relatively uniform. The language of these inscriptions is a standardized form of Luwian propagated by the Hittite kings at Hattusa and imitated by the Neo-Hittite rulers (see Yakubovich 2010a: 72–73). The uniformity of the inscriptions also suggests that the writing system continued to develop in close contact between these states, until it perished with the last of the Neo-Hittite states, ca. 700 B.C.E.

The subsequent paragraphs will provide a brief history of the states relevant to the texts offered in this volume. Apart from internal information from local hieroglyphic texts, the most important source for the history of the Neo-Hittite states are the Assyrian annals.

1.2.3. CILICIA

Cilicia plays an important role as a source of hieroglyphic inscriptions. There are two major texts from this area, both Phoenician-Luwian bilinguals. One of them, the inscription KARATEPE 1, is the longest preserved Luwian and Phoenician inscription to date. Cilicia is situated between the Taurus Mountains in the northwest, the Amanus Mountains in the east and the Mediterranean Sea in the south; it was of strategic importance, controlling Anatolian access to Syria. During the Bronze Age, it was populated by Hurrians and Luwians, its main city Adana is attested as Ataniya. Iron Age Hieroglyphic inscriptions speak of the city as Adana(wa), Phoenician '*dn*, while the Assyrian annals distinguish two regions, the Cilician plain or Que, and rough Cilicia or Hilakku. The Old Testament records that King Solomon traded horses with the kings of Que: "Also Solomon's import of horses was from Egypt and Kue, and the king's merchants procured them from Kue for a price" (1 Kgs 10:28; also 2 Chr 1:16); however, it remains questionable whether these passages refer to this Neo-Hittite state.[3] Assyrian sources first mention Cilicia in the year 858 B.C.E., and provide many references, most important among these is Sargon's II control of both Que and Hilakku. Neo-Babylonian and Classical sources provide further information for later periods.

Archaeological investigations, meanwhile, have little to contribute, the main excavation site is Karatepe, which, besides its valuable inscription, preserves archaeological structures, namely, a small fortress, two city gates, and walls. According to the hieroglyphic texts, the main Iron Age city was Adana, but because of continued settlement there, excavation is not likely. There are only very few indigenous inscriptions from Iron Age Cilicia, and these attest two generations of rulers based at Adana, a King Awarikus/Warikas of the house of Muksas (possibly classical Mopsus), and his successor, the regent Azatiwadas. Both names have possible equations in Assyrian annals, Awarikus as Urikki of Que, attested for the years 738–732, and 710–709, and Azatiwadas as Sanduarri, king of Kundi and Sissu, attested for the year 676 B.C.E.

1.2.4. KARKAMIŠ

Already an important seat of power under the Hittite Empire, Karkamiš survived the political changes at the end of the Bronze Age without obvious disruption. Karkamiš occupies a strategic position at an important crossing of the river Euphrates, and during the Bronze Age, controlled the Hittite territories in northern Syria. For biblical references to Karkamiš, see Jer 46:2; 2 Chr 35:20; Isa 10:9. A wealth of Hieroglyphic Luwian inscriptions originates from here, dating to between the eleventh and ninth centuries B.C.E. In 717 B.C.E., Karkamiš was annexed by the Assyrians, and finally, in 605 B.C.E., destroyed by Nebuchadrezzar.

---

3. Cf. Tadmor 1961.

In modern times, the site of Karkamiš was first identified in 1876 by George Smith, and representatives of the British Museum recovered important monuments from 1878–1881. Archaeological excavations took place between 1911–1914 until the outbreak of World War I, resuming in 1920, conducted by a British team led by Sir Leonard Woolley. Excavations were several times interrupted by warfare, and for many decades the site lay abandoned as the Syro-Turkish border runs through it. Very recently, the area has been cleared of land mines and excavations resumed in the autumn of 2011. To date, Karkamiš provides the greatest number of hieroglyphic inscriptions and sculpture of any single site.

Past archaeological work includes a survey of the fortifications and the excavation of two main areas, namely, the upper levels of the citadel, and the area of the lower town underneath, where most inscriptions and sculpture were found. Amongst important structural remains are a temple of the Storm God, the King's Gate and the Great Staircase ascending to the citadel.

The sculpture from Karkamiš offers dating criteria, while indigenous inscriptions attest several royal families. A line descending from the Hittite king Suppiluliuma I, who installed his son Piyassili/Šarri-Kušuḫ as Hittite viceroy and king of Karkamiš in ca. 1340 B.C.E., seems to have continued unbroken for at least five generations, unperturbed by the fall of the Hittite Empire. Nonetheless, Karkamiš lost its power over the former Hittite province of Syria and was reduced to a city-state. Karkamiš continued to retain its independence until the Assyrian conquest in 717 B.C.E. Assyrian annals only attest two kings of Karkamiš, Sangara (ca. 870–848) and Pisiri (ca. 738–717 B.C.E.), yet, unfortunately, these cannot currently be reconciled with any of the kings known from Luwian inscriptions; the latter confirm three native dynasties. The earliest is an archaic group using the by then vacant Hittite title of Great King, possibly because of a dynastic claim to the royal house of Hatti. Of these early kings, we know the following by name: Kuzi-Teššub, X-pa-ziti, Ura-Tarhunza and Tudhaliya(?). Next came the House of Suhis with its rulers Suhis I, Astuwalamanzas[4], Suhis II, and Katuwas, who ruled before 870 B.C.E. Also attested is a House of Astiruwas, named after a king called Astiruwas, who was succeeded by the regent Yariris, then Kamanis (son of Astiruwas), [a gap?], Sasturas, Sasturas's son (name not preserved). The house of Astiruwas falls within the gap between Sangara and Pisiri, thus possibly ruling ca. 848–738 B.C.E.

---

4. Previously read Astuwatamanzas; following the new readings of Yakubovich and Rieken (2010) this should be amended to Astuwalamanzas.

1.2.5. TELL AHMAR

Tell Ahmar is known from Assyrian sources as Til-Barsip, from hieroglyphic inscriptions as Masuwari. It is situated on the east bank of the river Euphrates, some 20 km south of Karkamiš, and holds a strategic position as a Euphrates crossing point. Šalmaneser III took the city in 856 B.C.E. from an Aramean ruler, Ahuni of Bit-Adini, and renamed it Kar-Šalmaneser. It is not entirely clear how long Til-Barsip had been in the hands of the Arameans, however, Luwian control of the site clearly predated this. There are archaeological remains of buildings resembling the style of nearby Karkamiš, destroyed by fire; sculptural remains, too, show stylistic links with Karkamiš, in particular with the Suhis-Katuwas period (tenth to early-ninth century B.C.E.). Both stele fragments and orthostat blocks used to build stone walls remain.

The inscriptions attest a ruling house with two competing lines. The first two kings belonged to the family of Hapatilas; next the family of Hamiyatas provided three kings, until finally power reverted back to the last descendant of Hapatilas's family. Unfortunately, his name is not preserved. An open question is how the author of the inscription ALEPPO 2 (see below, 2.4.4), a certain Arpas, fits into all of this.

1.2.6. MARAŞ

The Neo-Hittite state of Maraş also shows close links with Karkamiš, and its rulers may have been linked to the Hittite royal house via the line of Tarhuntassa. Indigenous inscriptions all stem from the ninth century B.C.E. Assyrian sources refer to a land Gurgum with its capital Marqas in the period 870–711 B.C.E., after which the area became an Assyrian province. There is very little archaeological data on the ancient state of Maraş, as no excavations or surveys have been undertaken. Luwian inscriptions speak of Maraş as the "Kurkumaean city."

The inscription MARAŞ 1 provides a chronology with seven generations of rulers ca. 1000–800 B.C.E.; three of which can be identified with rulers known from Assyrian sources. Another inscription, MARAŞ 8, provides two further ancestors, yet we do no know whether they also ruled over Maraş. Thus, we can reconstruct the following dynasty: [Astu-waramanzas, Muwatalis,] Laramas I, Muwizis, Halparuntiyas I, Muwatallis, Halparuntiyas II, Laramas II, Halparuntiyas III. Of these, Muwatallis can be identified as Mutalli in Assyrian sources, mentioned for the year 858 B.C.E. as paying tribute to Šalmaneser III; Halparuntiyas II as Qalparunda, attested for the year 853 B.C.E. as submitting to Šalmaneser; Laramas II as Palalam; and Halparuntiyas III as Qalparunda, attested for the year 805 B.C.E. Assyrian sources further mention a king Tarhulara for the years 743, 738, 732 B.C.E. who was dethroned and killed by his son Mutallu in 717 B.C.E.

This crime was promptly avenged by the Assyrian king Sargon II, and Gurgum annexed.

1.2.7. Hama

The modern city of Hama appears in the bible as Hamath, in Assyrian texts as Amat/Ham(m)at. The Neo-Hittite state of Hama provides only a small group of inscriptions, but gained importance as the earliest site from which hieroglyphic inscriptions were known, as outlined above (1.1). Excavations took place under a Danish team from 1931–38 but did not unearth many inscriptions, although some twenty cuneiform tablets were found. Settlement seems to have continued unbroken from the Neolithic to the Islamic period. In the first millennium B.C.E., Luwian kings ruled over Hama until they were replaced by Aramaeans ca. 800 B.C.E. Apart from two early inscriptions (see 2.2.4), the texts from Hama were commissioned by two rulers, Urahilina[5] (known as Irhuleni in Assyrian annals, ca. 853–845 B.C.E.) and his son Uratamis (ca. 840–820 B.C.E.).

1.2.8. Tabal

From the state of Tabal comes the second largest group of hieroglyphic inscriptions, after Karkamiš. Tabal (biblical Tubal) is located in the southeast of the Anatolian plateau, bordering onto the Taurus mountains in the southeast, Melid in the east, Cilicia to the south and Phrygia to the northwest. Tabal consisted of various small city states. By the eighth century B.C.E. these had merged into two, Tabal proper (Assyrian Bit-Burutaš) to the north and Tuwana (classical Tyanitis) to the south. There is little archaeological data on ancient Tabal. The earliest indigenous inscriptions (KIZILDAĞ-KARADAĞ, BURUNKAYA) come from the west, and may date as early as shortly after 1200 B.C.E. In these, a king Hartapus and his father Mursili, possible descendants of the Hittite kings of Tarhuntassa, claim the Hittite title of Great King. No further inscriptions can be dated to the following centuries until the eighth century B.C.E.

One differentiates two groups of inscriptions, one from the south (Tuwana), which provides information on a three generation dynasty of Tuwana: Muwaharanis, Warpalawas (Assyrian Urballa, ca. 738–709 B.C.E.), Muwaharanis. The other group of inscriptions stems from the north (Tabal proper), and attests different rulers, among them the family of Tuwatis and his son Wasusarmas (Assyrian sources record the latter as Wassurme, ca. 738–730 B.C.E.), as well as other rulers such as Kurtis (Assyrian Kurti, attested for the years 718, 713

---

5. Previously read Urahilina. I follow Yakubovich (2010b: 396 n. 9), who analyses the name as Urahilina, Luw. "(having) a great gate."

B.C.E.?). A particularly late writing style from Tabal is shown by the KULULU lead documents.

Assyrian control of Tabal was less firm than on other regions, and particularly the death of Sargon destabilized their hold over this area. The end of the indigenous hieroglyphic tradition therefore seems not to be due to Assyrian annexation but must have had other reasons. Assyrian texts mention Tabal for a last time in 651 B.C.E. Centuries later it reemerges in classical sources under the name of Cappadocia.

1.3. BIBLICAL HITTITES

It is for purely historical reasons that we speak of "Hittites" and the "Hittite" language. The Hittites spoke of themselves as "people of the land of Hatti" (the name given to it by earlier residents of the area, the Hattians), and called their language "Nesite" after the city Kaneš. But by the time the first remains of this civilization were rediscovered by modern scholars, any knowledge of the Hittite Empire had long vanished, and as mentioned above (1.1), the emerging, forgotten civilization was soon linked to *Ḥet, ha-ḥittî, ḥittîm* and *ḥittiyyot*. References in recently deciphered ancient Egyptian and Assyrian texts to a land of *ḫt'* or *Kheta* (Egyptian) or *Ḫatti* (Assyrian) seemed to confirm the link, and the term "Hittite" is still in use today.

Meanwhile, the question remains how the biblical Hittites fit into what we now know of the Hittite Empire and her successor states. The biblical Hittites do not form one homogenous group. At minimum, one can differentiate between Hittites within and outside of Palestine in the biblical references. Most references are to Palestinian Hittites, while only five passages refer to Hittites outside of Palestine. The land of these Hittites is shown to extend from the Euphrates to the Mediterranean Sea (Jos 1:2–4; Judg 1:26 refers to the same country), an area that includes the territory of the Neo-Hittites states in Syria and southern Anatolia. The "Kings of the Hittites" who traded in horses and cavalry (1 Kgs 10:29; 2 Chr 1:17; 2 Kgs 7:6) must therefore refer to Neo-Hittite kings, and the Hittite wives of Solomon (1 Kgs 11:1) should also be placed in this context. An inscription of the Assyrian King Šalmaneser III attests to contact between Neo-Hittites and Israelites, naming Irhuleni of Hamath and Ahab of Israel as allies of an anti-Assyrian alliance whom he defeated at the Battle of Qarqar in 853 B.C.E. This suggests a living memory of at the very least the Neo-Hittites of Syria among the authors of Old Testament scriptures during the ninth century B.C.E., and presumably thereafter.

But the majority of biblical references to the Hittites show them as natives of Canaan (e.g., Gen 15:19–21; Josh 3:10 refer to the Hittites as a tribe of Palestine; Gen 10:15 states that Heth is a son of Canaan). There is no conclusive evidence that can reconcile this group with any sucessors of the Hittite Empire. Another possibility would be that the Hittites entered the biblical text as an ideological and literary construct, keeping alive the memory of the historical Hittites. A final option would be that these Hittites were an immigrant group, possibly arriving in Palestine after the fall of the Hittite Empire, yet there is no material evidence for this, nor a convincing explanation why such immigrants should be perceived as indigenous.[6]

1.4. The Hieroglyphic Script

The hieroglyphic script is used to record the Luwian language with the help of pictorial signs. These are written "boustrophedon" or "as the ox ploughs," alternating their direction from line to line. In structure if not in appearance, the writing system closely resembles the cuneiform script, distinguishing likewise three different sign types, logograms, determinatives, and syllabograms. A logogram represents an entire word with just one picture. In its simplest form, the glyph depicts the object drawn but it may also depict an object associated with the intended word, such as the king's hat as a symbol for the king, or a word of similar sound. Determinatives are signs used to mark words as belonging to a specific sphere, maybe comparable to using titles such as Mr. and Mrs. to signify gender, but extending to a number of categories. Many of these we can understand while the logic of others eludes us. Syllabic signs are used to represent the sound of the word written with them; in the hieroglyphic writing system, these phonetic signs have the structure vowel (V), consonant-vowel (CV) or consonant-vowel-consonant-vowel (CVCV); a very small number of signs appears not to adhere to this pattern. Logograms and syllabic signs may be used exclusively or in combination, thus a word could be written with the logogram—with or without a phonetic complement, that is, the word end spelled phonetically—with logogram and full phonetic writing or written purely with phonetic signs. This type of writing poses one particular problem to modern readers: the practice of logographic writing may hide the underlying Luwian term, either partially or completely. Some signs may have either a logographic or phonetic reading, and, accordingly, have to be interpreted in the context in which they occur.

Visually, the script is called hieroglyphic because it depicts objects, some of which we can easily identify while others still defy recognition. The majority of hieroglyphic Luwian inscriptions survives on monuments of stone, and

---

6. For recent discussions of the subject, see Gerhards 2009; Collins 2007; Singer 2006.

there we find two ways of writing: either the signs were incised into a smooth surface, or the background was chiselled away so that the signs appear in relief. Among the signs themselves one can differentiate two shapes, a more pictorial, formal shape, and a more linear, cursive one. Scholars interpret the latter as a sign of increased handwritten usage, in the same way that the Egyptians used cursive hieroglyphs on papyrus. That the cursive sign forms that appear on stone monuments reflect the handwritten variant of the script is born out by the few surviving handwritten documents. Mainly, these are inscribed strips of lead. But as very little is preserved outside of the corpus of monumental stone inscriptions, the development of the script as a handwritten medium is, unfortunately, largely lost to us.

Earliest systematic writing can be dated to the fourteenth century B.C.E., when Hittite official and royal seals recorded names and titles with the hieroglyphic script. By the thirteenth century B.C.E., if not before,[7] inscriptions were written in hieroglyphic Luwian. While new inscriptions are still found today, the corpus of Bronze Age texts is, on the whole, not very large, and the surviving longer inscriptions date to the Late Empire period, especially to the last two generations of Hittite kings, Tudhaliya IV (ca. 1237–1209) and Suppiluliuma II (ca. 1205–?). Yet it is after the fall of the Empire, during the Iron Age, that the hieroglyphic script reaches its zenith. Inscriptions became much more numerous, often longer, and the writing system itself continued to develop, too.

The script evolved over the centuries of its usage, and this includes changes both in appearance and writing conventions. For instance, early texts are predominantly written with logograms, using a limited amount of phonetic signs, while later texts prefer phonetic writing, and are also more likely to use cursive sign forms. Individual sign shapes show innovation and change, too. The move away from predominantly logographic writing meant that more signs were used, and this way of writing is very helpful to the modern scholar trying to read these texts, as it records much if not all of the phonetic shape of words, making possible a better understanding of the language. By ca. 1100 B.C.E., when the texts regularly recorded grammatical endings, many phonetic spellings and syntactical features such as particle chains, the script is considered fully developed.[8]

---

7. This rests mainly on the dating of one object, the ANKARA silver bowl. For a new attempt a reconciling the problems of dating this object, see Durnford 2010.

8. For further discussion of the hieroglyphic script, see Hawkins 2000: 3–6; 2003: 155–59).

1.5. Hieroglyphic Scholarship

The surviving corpus of hieroglyphic Luwian inscriptions has grown steadily since the initial findings by Burckhardt and others in Syria, with texts originating from both Syria and Anatolia. Early on, newly deciphered texts from Babylon and Egypt provided some context, confirming the existence of a great Hittite Empire in this area. A first corpus of Hieroglyphic texts was published by Leopold Messerschmidt between 1900 and 1906, which included thirty-two major and twenty-nine minor texts, and a collection of epigraphs and seals. Yet early attempts to decipher the script were not very successful, and it is worth emphasizing that they were made without a bilingual text of reasonable length or even linguistic context; the archives of the Hittite Empire were not discovered until 1906. There was only a mini bilingual, a problematic digraphic seal—that is, written in cuneiform and hieroglyphs—known as the TARKONDEMOS seal. A major breakthrough was the discovery of clay tablets in the archives of the Hittite capital Hattusa. These instantly provided much information on the Hittite Empire in easily readable Akkadian texts, and the decoding of the Hittite language provided the necessary linguistic background to proceed with the decipherment of the hieroglyphic script. Most unexpectedly, Hittite turned out to be an Indo-European language. The cuneiform tablets provided knowledge not only of Hittite but also of its Anatolian relatives Luwian and Palaic.

The corpus of hieroglyphic inscriptions continued to grow, major contributions came from archaeological campaigns in Karkamiš (1911–1914) and Tell Ahmar (1929–1931) on the Euphrates. The Boğazköy excavations produced several hundred seal impressions, some of them digraphic. Finally, decipherment attempts began to bear fruit. The language was seen to be similar but not identical to Hittite and Cuneiform Luwian. There were five scholars in particular who, independently, worked with the available material: Piero Meriggi, Ignaz Gelb, Emil Forrer, Helmuth Theodor Bossert, and Bedrich Hrozný. Between them, they correctly identified many logographic and syllabic signs and worked out a sketch of the grammar. Yet erroneous readings kept these early results unreliable.

A most important discovery was made in 1946, when Bossert and Halet Çambel found the long bilingual of KARATEPE. The Luwian-Phoenician bilingual consists of seventy-five clauses, and survives in several copies. It is still the longest Hieroglyphic inscription known today. This text enabled scholars to confirm provisional readings and establish new ones, although it was not straight away fully exploited to discard erroneous readings. However, it greatly contributed to the knowledge of vocabulary and language. Further material was provided by seal impressions found at Ras Šamra, ancient Ugarit in 1953 and 1954.

Emanuel Laroche, a French linguist, and the Italian scholar Piero Meriggi worked on the hieroglyphic script and published important study tools in the 1960s, a sign list (Laroche 1960), glossary (Meriggi 1962), and text corpus (1966; 1967; 1975). Both already acknowledged the affinity of the language recorded with the hieroglyphic script with Cuneiform Luwian, yet a few erroneous readings of crucial signs obscured its exact relationship to Luwian and Hittite. In particular Bossert and Hermann Mittelberger began to question the reading of specific signs. Finally, certain readings were corrected with the help of new material in the shape of inscribed pithoi from Altıntepe. These new readings were announced in 1973 and published in 1974 in a joint article by John David Hawkins, Anna Morpurgo Davies, and Günter Neumann, and are now generally accepted. Since then, our understanding of the language has continued to grow, and recent years have seen several important additions to study tools such as the final publication of the KARATEPE bilingual by Halet Çambel, Hawkins's Corpus of Iron Age Inscriptions, and a volume on the Luwians edited by Craig Melchert, to name but a few. New text finds and insights keep this subject very dynamic, yet at the same time many open questions remain.

For instance, why was a new script invented at a time and among people who already wrote cuneiform? As long as the very beginnings of the hieroglyphic script remain obscure, we can only speculate, but it is impossible not to. There are four main differences between cuneiform and the hieroglyphic script: cuneiform is an abstract script, an international medium that came to Anatolia as an outside, foreign script invention, and was mainly used for administrative purposes on clay tablets. The hieroglyphs, meanwhile, are a pictorial, local script and an autochthonous script invention. They mainly survive on monuments, used for commemoration or display.

If we compare the two scripts and consider their advantages and disadvantages, we note several points in favor of the hieroglyphic script: As an autochthonous script invention they carried prestige. Inventing a writing system is clearly a great achievement, as we know by the reaction to different script inventions in history. It is quite possible that the script was a symbol of power, either as an intentional comparison with mighty Egypt, or at least with other peoples who had invented scripts. Further, using the script on monuments is a way of presenting oneself. The hieroglyphs, rooted as they are in the Hittite artistic tradition, are an expression of how the Hittites wanted to see themselves, and might additionally have been one means of forging an identity within a multi-ethnic state. And last but not least, picture-signs have the advantage of directly communicating with the onlooker, offering a level of recognition even to people who cannot read. While such a person would not have understood the text itself, he may have recognized common elements such as the names of gods, kings, and cities, and thus would have had at least minimal access to the text.

Undeniably, there are also disadvantages. Effective communication with this script was only possible between trained scribes—of which there would have been, at least initially, far fewer than cuneiform scribes. This was certainly a contributing factor why the script did not spread on an international level. Also, in comparison to cuneiform, the hieroglyphic script is badly suited to recording final consonants or consonant clusters, as it lacks the category of vowel-consonant signs. And clearly, the script was more difficult to draw than abstract cuneiform, and especially, to carve into stone.

1.6. Texts

The surviving hieroglyphic text corpus divides into two periods, Bronze and Iron Age. The majority of texts stem from the Iron Age. The few longer inscriptions from the Bronze Age pose added difficulties, for instance, they use a high number of logographic writings and add few grammatical endings, which makes them considerably harder to understand. Hieroglyphic inscriptions are conventionally named after their place of origin (in capital letters), and in the case of several inscription from one place, they are also numbered. As mentioned above, the great majority of inscriptions survive on stone monuments because the material is very durable. We know that hieroglyphs were also used in less formal contexts on other materials, but only very few examples of this type of usage have survived. In particular, this means that most of the extant text corpus is limited to a few literary genres. Commemorative, dedicatory, and building inscriptions abound, whereas private communication is almost extinct. This also limits the historical value of these texts, since many revert to recurring topoi and standard formulae. While this is testimony to the authors identifying with and continuing an ongoing tradition, it often provides disappointingly little information.

1.7. Kingship: Religion and Power

A few more words on the position of the king seem to be in order, since many of the preserved inscriptions were commissioned by rulers, and often portray the person of the king, and also his relationship with various deities. Where applicable, this will be also commented on below. Every king had personal gods with whom he maintained a close relationship; indeed, a typical form of representation since the Empire period shows the king in the embrace of his personal deity (e.g., on the rock reliefs of Yazılıkaya). Frequently, kings named the head of the Luwian pantheon, the Storm God Tarhunza, as their chief personal god. They acted as his representative on earth, holding supreme power among men, as the Storm God did among gods. Often, the king would call himself the servant of the Storm God, "beloved" by him, and by other gods, too. Kingship was justified by divine appointment, one often encounters the phrase "he/they (one or several gods) gave me my paternal succession." This implies both a system of hereditary, dynastic rule and of divine entitlement. The former could be overturned, as numerous interdynastic struggles and usurpations attest, while the latter would generally be claimed by the successful occupant of the throne. Kings played a central role in organized religion, from instigating the cult of a particular god, allocating regular provisions for a specific deity to performing in a ritual ceremony. But religion was only one aspect of ancient Near Eastern kingship. The king also represented supreme power in both military and judicial affairs. Neither is, of course, surprising, and we find many references to both in the hieroglyphic texts. Kings claimed military success—often expressed as the result of divine favour and preferment (see., e.g., 2.4.3). War, however, was not the only means of demonstrating strength and power, related subjects that frequently recur are hunting—the equivalent to warfare in times of peace—and building activities. The latter comprise urban architecture as a symbol of wealth and position, religious monuments and the building of fortresses, strengthening of borders and resettlement of depopulated areas, concluding and possibly crowning a successful military campaign. Judging by the number of inscriptions set up to commemorate some kind of building activity, sometimes in conjunction with establishing a cult, this was certainly a very important aspect of Neo-Hittite kingship. Finally, we infer that the king would have been the uppermost judicial authority, as he was during the Hittite Empire period. There is little concrete evidence for this as no archives of legal documents survive, yet there is one phrase that is encountered very frequently: many positive statements about the king are introduce with "because of my justice" (the gods loved me, etc.). Clearly, justice is an important constituent of kingship, and would qualify the king for the position of chief lord of justice. And not only did kings pride themselves in being just, they would also, occasionally, show mercy, for instance by exiling offenders rather than reverting to more draconian measures (see, e.g., 2.3.5).

2. TEXTS

This chapter offers a selection of Iron Age inscriptions in translation, according to genre. Bronze Age texts are excluded because they are considerably more complicated, which would necessitate a much higher degree of explanation and speculation. I have arranged the texts in groups: Bilinguals, Funerary and Commemorative Inscriptions, Building Inscriptions, Dedicatory Inscriptions, and Miscellanea.[1] Each group is introduced with a few general remarks, and each text is preceded by relevant information on provenance, dating, and other points of interest.

The transliterations of the texts follow their standard editions but have been brought up-to-date. Please note that as our understanding of language and script improves, further changes to current readings may become necessary.[2] As mentioned above (1.4), hieroglyphic signs may function as logogram, determinative, or syllabogram.[3] The transliteration distinguishes these as follows: logograms are transliterated with a Latin term in capital letters, since the underlying Luwian word is not always known to us. For instance, the drawing of a foot is transliterated as PES. Compound logograms are separated by a full stop as in DEUS. DOMUS, "temple." Sometimes signs defy description: in these cases, the transliteration will state the sign's number in the sign list, for example, *424. Two abbreviations are used, NEG for the negative and REL for the relative pronoun. One Luwian term is used to transliterate the postposition or preverb *arha*, trans-

---

1. While individual genres are modern classifications and thus open to debate, grouping texts of a similar type together illustrates the literary range of the surviving text corpus well.

2. Note that the new readings proposed by Rieken and Yakubovich (2010) have not been adopted in transliteration, instead the possibility of an interpretation /IV/ is examined for every case individually. To indicate the hieroglyphic sign, it seemed more neutral and thus preferable to keep the traditional values of *319, ta_4/i_4 and *172, ta_5/i_5.

I transliterate sign *448 *zú* as per Melchert (1987: 202); sign *432 za_5 as per Yakubovich (2010: 81–83); sign *462+*ra/i* as *mara/i* following Hawkins 2004.

3. For an account of the script illustrated with hieroglyphic signs cf. Payne (2010: 5–8).

literated in cursive capitals, *ARHA*. There is a special hieroglyphic sign to mark a logogram, the transliteration shows this with inverted commas, for example, "OCCIDENS." If a sign is used as a determinative, that, marking the sphere of a specific word, it is transliterated in capital letters like a logogram but, additionally, placed in parentheses. Some determinatives such as the marker for divine names precede their referent word, whereas others follow it. Thus (DEUS) TONITRUS, "the Storm God" but *ni-ki-ma-sa*(REGIO), "the Land Nikima." One single determinative is not placed in brackets, the superscript character ^{I}, which marks personal names, for example, ^{I}*ka-tú-wa/i-sa*, "Katuwas." Syllabic signs are transliterated with small cursive characters, each sign separated from the next by a hyphen. Occasionally, syllabic signs are used as phonetic indicators, showing part of the phonetic form of a logogram to help identify the underlying word. Phonetic indicators are transliterated in cursive capitals, for example, OMNIS+*MI*, "*tanima/i-*," "all, every." Many syllabic signs may represent more than one vowel, indicated in transliteration by a forward slash, that is, the sign *wa/i* may be read as *wa* or *wi*.

If several signs share the same value, the variants are numbered in order of frequency; the most common variant, variant one, carries no number. Logograms use subscript numbers only, that is, NEG, NEG_2, NEG_3 whereas syllabic signs differentiate variants two and three with accents, as in cuneiform, before moving on to index numbers, that is, *sa, sá, sà, sa_4, sa_5*, etc. If the index shows the letter x rather than a number, the value has not been firmly established but remains a suggestion.

A few additional characters need explaining: a vertical bar at the beginning of a word indicates that the original text uses a sign marking the beginning of the word. Since there was a desire to avoid blank space for aesthetic reasons, texts also use as a space filler either the sign *450, *a*, or less frequently the sign *209, *i*, transliterated, respectively, with a prime -´ or a superscript -^{i}. An asterisked *a* at the end of a word indicates that the letter should be read at the beginning of the word, a practice called initial-*a*-final.[4] For instance a writing *wa/i-mu-*a* shows the writing order of the original inscription but in analysis needs to be understood as *a=wa=mu*.

Two vertical bars indicate the end of a line in the original inscription; line numbers, where applicable, are indicated in the column furthest to the left of the transliteration. For ease of reference, the texts are broken up into individual clauses, given as numbered paragraphs to the left of the transliteration. The separation into clauses is aided by sentence-introductory particles within the text but please note that this is a modern division. The original texts do not use punc-

---

4. For a discussion of this phenomenon see Hawkins 2003: 159–61.

tuation to mark the end of a sentence. Broken and damaged text is indicated as shown below.

⟨...⟩	text damaged
[...]	text broken
[sign]	text restored (as required by context and/or attested in parallel inscriptions)
<...>	erroneous omission
<<...>>	erroneous inclusion
?	uncertain reading
?!	highly uncertain reading
!	amended reading
X, x	unidentified sign or trace thereof

The translation of the texts will be annotated with footnotes. However, as it seemed appropriate neither to repeat the commentary of the respective text editions (listed under text publications) unnecessarily nor to mention every problematic aspect; the commentary given here should be regarded as a subjective selection of interesting points. I have, in general, attempted to include new research and ideas, which I hereby offer up for discussion. Please note that the translation does not aim to replicate original sentence structure but to render a readable English text. A few common translation problems are indicated in the following manner:

(word)	addition, needed to form a proper English sentence
word(?)	tentative translation
WORD	Luwian term, meaning unknown
...	text not translatable
⟨...⟩	text damaged
[...]	text broken
[word]	text restored (as required by context and/or attested in parallel inscriptions)

2.1. BILINGUALS

Only a few multilingual inscriptions with Hieroglyphic Luwian exist, and most of these are Phoenician-Luwian bilinguals. The following two have been selected because of their state of preservation, literary structure, and content.

2.1.1. KARATEPE 1

Scholars first visited the site of Karatepe-Arslantaş, ca. 130 km northeast of Adana, in 1946, and excavations began in 1947. The ancient site had two stone gates, each bearing a version of the Hieroglyphic and Phoenician text. Accordingly, the Luwian texts are distinguished as Hu. (Hieroglyphisch unten = Lower (North) Gate) and Ho. (Hieroglyphisch oben = Upper (South) Gate; the Phoenician text as A (or Phu. = Phönizisch unten), B (Pho. = Phönizisch oben) and C; the latter is a slightly differing version recorded on the statue of a god, placed within the upper gate.

The Luwian and Phoenician versions correspond to an exceedingly high degree, and the overall text is well preserved. Apart from one passage in Hu., the Hieroglyphic and Phoenician texts from the North Gate are complete, while the South Gate inscriptions are less-well preserved. With a total of seventy-five clauses, this building inscription with historical narrative remains the longest surviving Luwian inscription to date. It also significantly advanced the script's decipherment as it became the first-known full bilingual inscription.

Given the nature of the script, the Hieroglyphic text takes up much more space than the Phoenician version. Version Hu. stretches over many elements, ranging from ordinary stone blocks to ornamental pieces, covering the figures of a lion and a sphinx and appearing in between relief sculptures. These elements were not found in the natural reading order as established by the Phoenician text version. Copy Ho. was found scattered in no apparent order and survives in a fragmented state. Apart from the bilingual, three smaller Hieroglyphic inscriptions were found at Karatepe, without corresponding Phoenician versions, but as they only consist of two short sentences each, they will not be considered here.

The dating of the inscription has been much debated. It rests, on the one hand, on dating the historical figure of Awarikus, King of Adana and his successor, the ruler Azatiwadas. If Awarikus is correctly identified with Urikki of Que, known from Assyrian sources, we know that he ruled in 738–732 B.C.E. and was exiled in 710–709 B.C.E. This would date Azatiwadas's rule to the end of the eighth or the beginning of the seventh century B.C.E. On the other hand, the inscription can be dated by palaeographic and stylistic criteria. There is general agreement that the Phoenician script should be dated to the end of the eighth century B.C.E., and the Hieroglyphic script also argues for the later-eighth century B.C.E. For instance, it shows a tendency towards innovative phonetic signs. However, scholars disagree on the style of the monument, dating it to either the ninth or eighth century B.C.E.

The following transliteration shows both Hieroglyphic versions, Hu. and Ho., and, solely for reference, the most complete Phoenician version, Phu.[5] The translation combines the two text versions Hu. and Ho., and will only identify the copy where relevant. In this text, Azatiwadas, speaks to us of his good and beneficial deeds for Adana, which he effected in his role as ruler. He glorifies his times, highlights his intimate relationship with several gods, and, finally, invokes blessings, and curses potential offenders. The text shows signs of using deliberate stylistic devices, especially repetition and variation.[6] I have grouped the individual clauses in paragraphs forming a unit of sense, which often illustrates particular rhetorical figures of speech. The original text does not indicate paragraphs, and sentences only in so far as new clauses are introduced by specific particles used for this purpose.

§ 1   Hu.
       |EGO-*mi* ¹(LITUUS)*á-za-ti-i-wa/i-tà-sá* (DEUS SOL-*mi-sá* CAPUT-*ti-i-sá* (DEUS)TONITRUS-*hu-ta-sa* SERVUS-*ta₄/i₄-sá*

       Ho.
       EGO [...

       Phu/A I. 1–2
       '*nk 'ztwd hbrk b'l 'bd b'l*

§ 2   Hu.
       |*á-wa/i+ra/i-ku-sa-wa/i* || REL-*i-na* MAGNUS+*ra/i-nu-wa/i-ta á-*TANA-*wa/i-ní-i-sá*(URBS) REX-*ti-sá*

       Ho.
       [*á-w*]*á/í+ra/i-*[*ku*]-*sa-wa/i* [REL]-*i-na* [...-*w*]*a/i-ta á-*TANA-[*wa/i*]-*ní-*[...] (URBS) ‹REX›-*ti-sa*

       Phu/A I. 2
       '*š 'dr 'wrk mlk dnnym*

§ 3   Hu.
       wa/i-mu-u (DEUS)TONITRUS-*hu-za-sa á-*TANA-*wa/i-* ||*ia*(URBS) MATER-*na-tí-na tá-ti-ha i-zi-i-tà*

---

5. For the Phoenician text versions and their translation, see Röllig in Çambel 1999: 50–73. An integrated reading is offered by Lawson Younger (1998).

6. For an indepth analysis, see Payne, forthcoming.

Ho.

wá/í-mu [...]-*za-sa* [...

Phu/A I. 3

p'ln b'l ldnnym l'b wl'm

§ 4   Hu.

|ARHA-ha-wa/i |la+ra/i+a-nú-ha |á-TANA-wa/i-na(URBS)

Ho.

[...   ...](URBS)

Phu/A I. 3–4

yḥw 'nk 'yt dnnym

§ 5   Hu.

|"MANUS"(-)la-tara/i-ha-ha-wá/í |á-TANA-wá/í-za(URBS)
|"TERRA+X"(-)wá/í+ra/i-za |zi-na |("OCCIDENS")i-pa-mi
|VERSUS-ia-na |zi-pa-wá/í (ORIENS)ki-sà-ta-mi-i |VERSUS-na

Ho.

"MANUS"(-)la-tara/i-ha-ha-wà/ì |á-TANA-wa/i-za(URBS)
TERRA+LA+LA(-)wá/í+ra/i-za zi-na ("OCCIDENS")i-pa-mi
|‹VERSUS›-[...

Phu/A I. 4–5

yrḥb 'nk 'rṣ 'mq 'dn lmmṣ' šmš w'd mb'y

§ 6   Hu.

|á-mi-ia-za-há-wa/i ("DIES<")ha-lí-za |á-TANA-wá/í-ia(URBS) |OMNIS+MI-ma |("BONUS")sa-na-wa/i-ia
|("CORNU+RA/I")su+ra/i-sa |(LINGERE)ha-sa-sa-ha |á-sá-ta

Ho.

[...]OMNIS-‹MI›-ma BONUS-na-wá/í[...] |(LINGERE)ha-s[a-... ...-t]a

Phu/A I. 5–6

wkn bymty kl n'm ldnnym wšb' wmn'n

§ 7   Hu.

|("MANUS<">)su-wá/í-ha-ha-wá/í |pa-há+ra/i-wa/i-ní-zi (URBS) |(<">*255")ka-ru-na-zi

Ho.
[...]-*ha*+*ra/i-wa/i-n*[*í-z*]*i*(URBS) (*255)*ka-ru-na-zi*

Phu/A I. 6
wml' 'nk 'qrt p'r

§ 8 Hu.
|EQUUS.ANIMAL-*zú-ha-wa/i-ta* (EQUUS.ANIMAL)*á-zú-wa/i* |SUPER+*ra/i-ta* |*i-zi-i-ha*

Ho.
(EQUUS.ANIMAL)*á-‹zú›-pa-wá/í-ta* (EQUUS.ANIMAL) *á-zú-wá/í* SUPER+*ra/i-ta i-zi-i-ha*

Phu/A I. 6–7
wp'l 'nk ss 'l ss

§ 9 Hu.
EXERCITUS-*la/i/u-za-pa-wa/i-ta* |EXERCITUS-*la/i/u-ní* |SUPER+*ra/i-ta* |*i-zi-i-há*

Ho.
[...   ]-‹*lí*›[...   ]

Phu/A I. 7
wmgn 'l mgn

§ 10 Hu.
|(‹">SCUTUM")*hara/i-li-pa-wa/i-ta* |("SCUTUM")*hara/i-li* |SUPER+*ra/i-ta* |*i-zi-i-há* ‹...›

Ho.
[...]-*pa-wá/í-t*[*a*] |EXERCITUS-*la/i/u-ní-i* SUPER+*ra/i-ta* |*i-zi-i-ha* OMNIS-*MI-ma-z*[*a*] |(DEUS)TONITRUS-*hu-ta-tí* DEUS-*na-ri*+*i-ha*

Phu/A I. 7–8
wmḥnt 'l mḥnt b'br b'l w'lm

§ 11 Hu.
REL-*pa-wá/í* |(*255)*mara/i-ia-ní-zi* |ARHA |*ma-ki-sa-há* ||

Ho.
[...] |(*"255")*mara/i-i*[*a*]-*ní*[...

Phu/A I. 8
wšbrt mlṣm

§ 12 Hu.
|("MALUS₂")ha-ní-ia-ta-pa-wa/i-ta-´ |REL-ia |(TERRA)ta-sà-REL+ra/i |a-ta |á-sá-ta

Ho.
|("MALUS₂")há-ní-ia-ta-ia-pa-wa/i-ta REL-ia ("TERRA+LA+LA<">)wa/i+ra/i-ri+i a-ta |á-sa-ta-´

Phu/A I.
see § 13

§ 13 Hu.
|wá/í-ta (TERRA)ta-sà-REL+ra/i<-ri+i⁷> ARHA |‹*501›[...]-há

Ho.
|wa/i-ta ("TERRA")ta-sà-REL+ra/i-ri+i |ARHA *501-ha-há

Phu/A I. 9
wtrq 'nk kl hr' 'š kn b'rṣ

§ 14 Hu.
|á-ma-||za₄-há-wá/í-ta |DOMINUS-ní-za |DOMUS-na-za |(BONUS)sa-na-wá/í |u-sa-nú-há

Ho.
|á-ma-za-pa-wá/í-ta-´ DOMINUS-ní-za || [...

Phu/A I. 9–10
wyṭn' 'nk bt 'dny bn'm

§ 15 Hu.
|á-mi-há-wa/i |DOMINUS-ní-i |(NEPOS)ha-su-´ |OMNIS-MI-ma ||(BONUS)sa-na-wa/i-ia |CUM-na i-zi-i-há

Ho.
[...] |OMNIS-MI-ma-ia |("BONUS")sa-na-wá/í-ia |CUM-ni i-zi-i-há

Phu/A I. 10
wp'l 'nk lšrš 'dny n'm

§ 16   Hu.
|*á-pa-sá-há-wá/í-ta* |*tá-ti-i* |("THRONUS")*i-sà-tara/i-ti* ("SOLIUM[")*i*]-*s*[*à-nu-wa/i-ha*]

Ho.
|*á-pa-sa-há-wa/i-ta-´* |*tá-ti-i* |("THRONUS")*i-sà-tara/i-tí-i* |("SOLIUM")*i-sà-nu-wà/ì-há-´* ||

Phu/A I. 11
wyšb 'nk 'l ks' 'by

§ 17   [Hu.]

(Ho. lacks this clause).

Phu/A I. 11–12
wšt 'nk šlm 't kl mlk

§ 18   Hu.
[... || ...] |[*i-zi*]-*i*-[*ta*] |*á-*[*mi*]-*ia-ti* |IUSTITIA-*na-ti* |*á-mi-ia+ra/i-ha* |("COR")*á-ta-na-sa-ma-ti* |*á-mi-ia+ra/i-há* || |("BONUS")*sa-na-wa/i-sa-tara/i-ti*

Ho.
|OMNIS-*MI-sa-ha-wa/i-mu-ti-i* REX-*ti-sa* |*tá-ti-na* |*i-zi-tà* |*á-mi-tí* |IUSTITIA-*na-ri+i* |*á-mi-ia+ra/i-há* |"COR<">-*ta-na-sa-ma-ri+i* |*á-mi+ra/i-ha* |("BONUS")*sa-na-wa/i-sa-tara/i-tí*

Phu/A I. 12–13
w'p b'bt p'ln kl mlk bṣdqy wbḥkmty wbn'm lby

§ 19   Hu.
("CASTRUM")*ha+ra/i-ní-sà-pa-wá/í* |PUGNUS(-)*la/i/u-mi-tà-ia* ‹AEDIFICARE›-*MI-ha* [...

Ho.
ha+ra/i-ní-[|| ...] |("FINES")*i+ra/i-há-za*

Phu/A I. 13–14
wbn 'nk ḥn!yt 'zt bkl qṣyt 'l gblm

§ 20   Hu.
(MALUS)*á-tu-wa/i-ri+i-zi-wa/i-ta* |CAPUT-*tí-zi* |REL-*ta-na* |*a-ta* ‹*á-sa-ta*› ("*217?")*u-sa-lí-‹zi*›

Ho.

|MALUS-ta_4/i_4-zí-wá/í-ta-´ ᴵCAPUT-tí-i-zi |REL-i-ta-na a-ta |a-sa_4-ta |("*217")u-sà-lì-zí

Phu/A I. 14–15
bmqmm b'š kn 'šm r'm b'l 'gddm

§ 21 Hu.
NEG_2-wá/í REL-zi |SUB-na-na PUGNUS.PUGNUS-ta_4/i_4-ta |mu-ka-sa-sa-na |DOMUS-ní-i

Ho.
NEG_2-wa/i REL-zi |SUB-na-na |tà-tà-ta mu-ka-sá-sá-na || DOMUS-ní-i

Phu/A I. 15–16
'š bl 'š 'bd kn lbt mpš

§ 22 Hu.
á-mu-pa-wá/í-ma-tà |(LITUUS)á-za-ti-wa/i+ra/i-sá |("PES") pa-tà-za |SUB-na-na |PONERE-há

Ho.
|á-mu-pa-wa/i-ma-ara/i (LITUUS)á-za-ti-wa/i-tà-sá |("PES") pa-tà-za |SUB-na-na "PONERE"-há

Phu/A I. 16–17
w'nk 'ztwd štnm tḥt p'my

§ 23 Hu.
|REL-pa-wá/í-ta |LOCUS-ta_4/i_4-ta-za-´ |á-pa-ta-za |("CASTRUM")ha+ra/i-ní-sà |a-ta |AEDIFICARE+MI-ha

Ho.
|REL-i-pa-wa/i-ta |"LOCUS<">-ta_4/i_4-ta-za ||<á-pa-ta-za> (CASTRUM)ha+ra/i-ní-i-sà a-ta | || [...]

Phu/A I. 17
wbn 'nk ḥn¹yt bmqmm hmt

§24 Hu.
|á-TANA-wa/i-sa-wa/i(URBS) || |REL-ti |(BONUS)wa/i+ra/i-ia-ma-la |SOLIUM-MI-i

Ho.
[…] REL-*ti* |(BONUS)*wa/i+ra/i-ia-má-la* |SOLIUM+*MI-i*

Phu/A I. 17–18
lšbtnm dnnym bnḥt lbnm

§ 25   Hu.
|*274-*ta-li-ha-há-wa/i* "CASTRUM"-*sà* PUGNUS(-)*la/i/u-mi-tà-ia-´* || ("OCCIDENS")*i-pa-mi* "VERSUS"-*na*

Ho.
|(*274)*há-ta-li-há-há-wá/í* ("CASTRUM")*ha+ra/i-ní-sà* |PUGNUS(-)*la/i/u-mi-tà-iá* ("SOL")*i-pa-mí-i* |VERSUS-*na*

Phu/A I. 18–19
w'n 'nk 'rṣt 'zt bmb' šmš

§ 26   Hu.
|NEG$_2$-*wa/*i REL-*ia* (*274)*ha-ta-la-i-ta* |FRONS-*li-zi* REX-*ti-zi*

Ho.
|NEG$_2$-*wa/i* |REL-*ia* |(*274)*há-ta-*||*la-i-ta* |FRONS-*la/i/u-zí* REX-*zi*

Phu/A I. 19
'š bl 'n kl hmlkm

§ 27   Hu.
|*á-mu* || REL-*zi* |PRAE-*na* |*á-sá-ta*

Ho.
|*á-mu-wa/i* |REL-*zi*$_4$ |PRAE-*na* |*á-sá-ta*

Phu/A I. 19
'š kn lpny

§ 28   Hu.
|*á-mu-pa-wa/i+ra/i* (LITUUS)*á-za-ti-wa/i+ra/i-sá* (*274)*ha-ta-li-i-ha*

Ho.
|REL-*i-pa-wa/i-ara/i* |*á-mu* (OCULUS)*á-za-ti-wa/i-tà-sá-´*(*274)*ha-ta-li-há*

Phu/A I. 19–20
w'nk 'ztwd 'ntnm

§ 29 Hu.
INFRA-*ta-ha-wa/i-ta* || |("PES")*u-sá-ha*

Ho.
INFRA-*ta-ha-wa/i-ta* |("PES")*u-sa-há-´* ||

Phu/A I. 20
yrdm 'nk

§ 30 Hu.
INFRA-*ta-ha-wa/i-tà* |(SOLIUM)*i-sà-nú-há* (DEUS)ORIENS-*mi* VERSUS-*na á-mi-ia-za-ta* (FINES)*i+ra/i-há-za* ||

Ho.
[...] (DEUS)ORIENS-*mi* VERSUS-*na* |*á-mí-za-ta* |("FINES") *i-ra/i-ha-za*

Phu/A I. 20–21
yšbm 'nk bqṣt gbly bmṣ' šmš

§ 31 Hu.
REL-*pa-wa/i* |*á-TANA-wa/i-ní-zi*(URBS) |*zi-tà* |*á-pa-ti-i* INFRA-*ta* |(SOLIUM)*i-sà-nú-wa/i-ha*

Ho.
REL-*pa-wa/i* |*á-TANA-wa/i-ní-zi*(URBS)<<-*pa-wa/i*>> |*zi-tà* |*a-pa-ri+í* <INFRA-*ta*> (SOLIUM)*i-sà-nu-há*

Phu/A I. 21–II. 1
wdnnym yšbt šm

§ 32 Hu.
|*a-wa/i á-mi-za* |("DIES")*ha-li-ia-za* || |*á-TANA-wa/i-ní-zi*(URBS) FINES+*hi-zi* "MANUS"(-)*la-tara/i-ha* |*zi-na* |"OCCIDENS"-*pa-mi* |VERSUS-*ia-na* |*zi-pa-wa/i* "ORIENS"-*ta-mi* VERSUS-*na*

Ho.
|*a-wá/í* |*á-mi-ia-za* |("DIES")*ha-li-ia-za* || [...

Phu/A II. 1–3
wkn bymty bkl gbl 'mq 'dn lmmṣ' šmš w'd mb' y

§ 33 Hu.
|á-pa-ta-za-pa-||wa/i-ta |?"LOCUS"-ta₄/i₄-ta-za <<-ha-pa-wa/i>> |REL-ia HWI-sà-ta rú-wa/i-na |á-sa-ta

Ho.
[—]

Phu/A II. 3–4
wbmqmm 'š kn lpnm nšt'm

§ 34 Hu.
CAPUT-ti-sa-wa/i+ra/i REL-i-ta-na HWI-sà-i-ia || "VIA"-wa/i-na ("PES₂")i-u-na

Ho.
[—]

Phu/A II. 4–5
'š yšt' 'dm llkt drk

§ 35 Hu.
REL-pa-wa/i a-mi-ia-za ("DIES")há-li-ia-za |FEMINA-ti-zi-há "FUSUS"(-)si-tara/i<-?> PES₂.PES₂-tà-ti

Ho.
[—]

Phu/A II. 5–6
wbymty 'nk 'št tk lḥdy dl plkm b'br b'l w'lm

§ 36 Hu.
a-wa/i á-mi-ia-za || (DIES)há-li-ia-za (CORNU+RA/I) su+ra/i-sá |(LINGERE)há-sá-sá-ha sa-na-wa/i-za-sa-ha |SOLIUM-MI-ia-sa |sá-ta

Ho.
[—]

Phu/A II. 7–8
wkn bkl ymty šb' wmn'm wšbt n'mt

§ 37 Hu.
|BONUS+*RA*/*I*-*ia*-*ma*-*la*-*ha*-*wa*/*i* SOLIUM-*MI*-*ta* |*á-TANA-wa/i-sá*(URBS) ‖ |*á-ta-na-wa/i-za-ha*(URBS) |TERRA+*LA*+*LA-za*

Ho.
[—]

Phu/A II. 8–9
wnḥt lb ldnnym wlkl 'mq 'dn

§ 38 Hu.
|*a-wa/i za* "CASTRUM"-*zá* AEDIFICARE+*MI-ha*

Ho.
[—]

Phu/A II. 9
wbn 'nk hqrt z

§ 39 Hu.
wa/i-tu-ta (LITUUS)*á-za-ti-wa/i-tà-ia-na*(URBS) |*á-ta₄/i₄-*‖*ma-za* PONERE-*ha*

Ho.
[—]

Phu/A II. 9–10
wšt 'nk šm 'ztwdy

§ 40 Hu.
REL-*pa-wa/i-mu* POST-*na* |(DEUS)TONITRUS-*hu-za-sá* (DEUS)CERVUS₂-*za-sá-há* |*sá-ta za-ti* "CASTRUM"-*si* AEDIFICARE-*MI-na*

Ho.
[—]

Phu/A II. 10–11
k b'l wršp ṣprm šlḥn lbnt

§§ 41–47 missing in Ho., fragmentary in Hu.

§ 41	Hu.
	[...]-tà [AEDIFI]CARE-*MI-ha* [...]-ta[...
	Ho.
	[—]
	Phu/A II. 11–14
	wbny 'nk b'br b'l wb'br ršp ṣprn! bšb' wbmn'm wbšbt n'mt wbnḥt lb
§§ 42–43	no fragments of Hu. or Ho. identified
	Phu/A II. 14–16
	lkny mšmr l'mq 'dn wlbt mpš
	k bymty kn l'rṣ 'mq 'dn šb' wmn'm
§ 44	Hu.
	[...]x[...]*i-zi-i-*[...] |*á-mi-*[*ia-za*] |("DIES")*ha-li-*[*ia*]*-z*[*a*]
	Ho.
	[—]
	Phu/A II. 16–17
	wbl kn mtm ldnnym ll bymty
§ 45	Hu.
	|*z*[*a-pa*/*ha-wa/i*]-´ <">CASTRUM"-*sà-z*[*á*] |AEDIFICARE-*M*[*I*]*-ha*
	Ho.
	[—]
	Phu/A II. 17
	wbn 'nk hqrt z
§ 46	not in Hu.; Ho. missing
	Phu/A II. 17–18
	št 'nk šm 'ztwdy
§ 47	Hu.
	|*wa/i-t*[*a*...] *z*[*a*$_4$-...] |(DEUS)TONI[TRUS ...] *a-ta* (SOLIUM) *i-s*[*à*]*-nú-ha*

Ho.
[... ...]-sà-nú-há

Phu/A II. 18–19
yšb 'nk bn b'l krntryš

§ 48   Hu.
wa/i-na |i-zi-sa-tu-na ta-ia ("FLUMEN")há-pa+ra/i-sá |OMNIS-MI-i-sá |(ANNUS)u-si mara/i BOS.ANIMAL-sá (*486)REL-tu-na-ha (OVIS.ANIMAL)há-wa/i-sá |"VITIS"(-)há+ra/i-ha OVIS.ANIMAL-wa/i-sa

Ho.
wá/í-na i-zi-i-sa-tú-na CRUS-ia |FLUMEN-pari-i-sá |OMNIS-MI-i-sá |("ANNUS")u-si |("ANNUS")mara/i-i |(BOS.ANIMAL)wa/i-wa/i-sa ("*486")REL-tú-na-ha |("OVIS.ANIMAL<">)há-wa/i-sá |"VITIS"(-)há<+ra/i>-wá/í |(OVIS.ANIMAL)há-wá/í-i-sá

Phu/A II. 19–Phu/A III. 2
wylk zbḥ lkl hmskt zbḥ ymm 'lp 1 wb['t ḥ]rš š 1 wb't qṣr š 1

§ 49   Hu.
wa/i-ta u-sa-nú-wa/i-tu-u (LITUUS)á-za-ti-wa/i-tà-na sa-pi-sá-ta$_5$/i$_5$-ri+i |ha-tà+ra/i-ti-i-há

Ho.
[wa/i-ta u-sa-nu]-wá/í-tú-u (OCULUS)á-za$_4$-ti-wá/í-tà-na |sá-pi-sa-ara/i-ri+i ha-IUDEX+RA/I-ri+í-há

Phu/A III. 2–3
wbrk b'l kr[n]tryš 'yt 'ztwd ḥym wšlm

§ 50   Hu.
SUPER+ra/i-li-há-wa/i-sá |FRONS-la/i/u-sá i-zi-ia+ra/i-ru |OMNIS-MI-wa-za REX-ta-za

Ho.
|SUPER+ra/i-lí-ha-wa/i-sá |FRONS-li-i-sá i-zi-ia-rú |OMNIS-MI-ní-i-ma-za$_4$ |REX-tá-za

Phu/A III. 4
w'z 'dr 'l kl mlk

§ 51 Hu.
pi-ia-tu-há-wa/i-tu-u (DEUS)TONITRUS-*hu-za-sá*
ARHA *u-sa-nú-wa/i-mi-sá za-si-há-wa/i* |("CASTRUM")
há<+ra/i>-na-sá-si DEUS-*ní-zi* (LITUUS)*á-za-ti-wa/i-tà-ia* ||
"LONGUS"-*ta₅/i₅-ia* (DIES)*há-li-ia mi-ia-ti-zi-ha* || (ANNUS)
u-si-zi sa-na-wa/i-sá-ha-wa/i || *tá-mi-hi-sá*

Ho.
|*pi-iá-tù-há-wa/i-tu₄-u* (DEUS)TONITRUS-*huₓ-za₄-sa*
|ARHA |(BONUS)*u-sa-nú-wá/í-mí-sá za-i¦-si-i-hǎ-wá/í* ||
("CASTRUM")*há+ra/i-ní-sà-si* |DEUS-*SA₄-zi* ¹(OCULUS)
á-za-tí-wá/í-tà-ia ("LONGUS")*a+ra/i-ia* |("DIES")*há-li-iá*
|*mì-ia-tí-zi₄-há* |ANNUS-*si-zi* |(BONUS)*sa-na-wà/ì-sa-há-wá/í*
|*tá-mi-hi-sá*

Phu/A III. 4–6
ltty b'l krntryš wkl 'ln qrt l' ztwd 'rk ymm wrb šnt wrš' t n'mt

§ 52 Hu.
|*pi-ia-tu-há-wa/i-tu* OMNIS-*MI-ma-za* || <*pihas-sa tanimanza*>
REX-*za* SUPER+*ra/i-ta*

Ho.
pi-ià-tù-há-wá/í-tú OMNIS-*MI-ma-za-´* "FULGUR"-*há-sá*
OMNIS-*MI-za* |REX-*ta-za* SUPER+*ra/i-ta*

Phu/A III. 6–7
w-'z 'dr 'l kl mlk

§ 53 Hu.
REL-*pa-wa/i za* ("CASTRUM")*há+ra/i-ní-sà-*||*za i-zi-ia-ru*
(DEUS)BONUS-*sa* (DEUS)VITIS-*sá-há*

Ho.
|REL-*i-pa-wà/ì* |*za-´* [...||...] (DEUS)VITIS-*tí-ti-há*

Phu/A III. 7
wkn hqrt z b'lt šb' wtrš

§ 54 Hu.
REL-*pa-wa/i-ta* || |REGIO-*ní-ia* REL-*ia a-ta* |SOLIUM+*MI-sá-i*

Ho.

|REL-*pa-wá/í-ta* REGIO-*iá* <REL-*ia*> *a-ta* |(SOLIUM)*i-sà-nú-wa/i-ti*

Phu/A III. 7–8

w'm z 'š yšb bn

§ 55　Hu.

wa/i-tà i-zi-ia-rú OVIS.ANIMAL-*wa/i-si* BOS.ANIMAL-*wa/i-si* (DEUS)BONUS-*si* (DEUS)VITIS-*ia-si-há*

Ho.

|*wá/í-tà* |*i-zi-ia-rú* |OVIS.ANIMAL-*wa/i-si* |BOS.ANIMAL-*si* |(DEUS)BONUS-*sa* (DEUS)"VITIS"-*ia-si-há*

Phu/A III. 8–9

ykn b'l 'lpm wb'l ṣ'n wb'l šb' wtrš

§ 56　Hu.

|*ma-wa/i-za* |*ha-sá-tu-´*

Ho.

|*ma-wá/í-za* |*ha-sa-tù*

Phu/A III. 9

wbrbm yld

§ 57　Hu.

ma-pa-wa/i MAGNUS+*ra/i-nú-wa/i-tu-´*

Ho.

|*ma-pa-wá/í* MAGNUS+*ra/i-nú-wa/i-tu*

Phu/A III. 10

wbrbm y'dr

§ 58　Hu.

ma-pa-wa/i (CRUX)*pa+ra/i-na-wa/i-tu-u* (LITUUS)*á-za-ti-wa/i-tà-ia mu-ka-sa-sá-há-´* DOMUS-*ní-i* (DEUS)TONITRUS-*hu-ta-*[*ti*] DEUS-*na-ti-há*

Ho.
|*ma-pa-wá/í* ("DOMUS.CRUX")*pa+ra/i-na-wa/i-tu*$_4$
(OCULUS)*á-za-ti-wá/í+ra/i-ia mu-ka-sá-sa-há* |(DOMUS)
pa+ra/i-ní ‖ […]

Phu/A III. 10–11
wbrbm yʻbd l'ztwd wlbt mpš bʻbr bʻl w'lm

§ 59 Hu.
REX-*ta-ti-i-pa-wa/i* REL+*ra/i* REL-*sa-há* ‖

Ho.
[—]

Phu/A III. 12
w'm mlk bmlkm

§ 60 Hu.
ní-pa-wa/i-sa ¹CAPUT-*ti-sá*

Ho.
[—]

Phu/A III. 12
wrzn brznm

§ 61 Hu.
¹CAPUT-*ti-ia-za-ha-wa/i-tu-ta á-ta*$_4$/*i*$_4$-*ma-za*

Ho.
[—]

Phu/A III. 12–13
'm 'dm 'š 'dm šm

§ 62 Hu.
|*za* |*á-sa*$_5$-*za-ia*

Ho.
[—]

(Phu.: nothing corresponding)

§ 63

Hu.
ARHA-wa/i-ta "*69"(-)i-ti-wa/i || (LITUUS)á-za-ti-wa/i-tà-sá á-ta₅/i₅-ma-za PORTA-la-na-ri+i zi-na

Ho.
[...]|á-ta₄/i₄-ma-za₄ "PORTA"-na zi-na

Phu/A III. 13–14
'š ymḥ šm 'ztwd bš'r z

§ 64

Hu.
wa/i-mu-ta || á-ma-za á-ta₄/i₄-ma-za a-ta tu-pi-wa/i

Ho.
[—]

Phu/A III. 14
wšt šm

§ 65

Hu.
ni-pa-wa/i-sá (COR)á-la/i/u-na-za-ia "CASTRUM<">-ní-si za-ti ||

Ho.
[...]-za-ia |"CASTRUM"-si [...]

Phu/A III. 14–15
'm 'p yḥmd 'yt ḥqrt z

§ 66

Hu.
wa/i-ta a-ta AEDIFICARE+MI-i "PORTA"-la-na za-ia

Ho.
[—]

Phu/A III. 15
wys' hš'r z

§ 67

Hu.
(LITUUS)á-za-ti-wa/i-tà-sa REL-ia i-zi-ta₅/i₅

Ho.
[—]

Phu/A III. 15–16
'š p'l 'ztwd

§ 68 Hu.
|a-wa/i za-ri+i |á-sa₅-za-ia

Ho.
[...]-ti-´[...]

(Phu.: nothing corresponding)

§ 69 Hu.
wa/i+ra/i-la-ia-wa/i "PORTA"-la-na i-zi-i-wa/i

Ho.
[...]-ia-[...]-na [...]-wa/i

Phu/A III. 16
wyp'l lš'r zr

§ 70 Hu.
|á-ma-z<a>-há-wa/i-mu-ta á-ta₄/i₄-ma-za-´ a-ta tu-pi-wa/i

Ho.
[... a-t]a [tu]-pi-wa/i

Phu/A III. 16
wšt šm 'ly

§ 71 Hu.
ní-wa/i-ta ("COR")á-la/i/u-na-ma-ti a-ta AEDIFICARE-MI-ri+i-i ||

Ho.
[ni-w]a/i-ta á-[la/i/u-na]-‹má-ti› [...]-MI-ti-i

Phu/A III. 17
'm bḥmdt ys'

§ 72a Hu.
ní-pa-wa/i MALUS-ta₄/i₄-sa-tara/i-ri+i ||

Ho.
ní-pa-wa/i || |MALUS-ta₄/i₄-sá-tara/i-ri+i

Phu/A III. 17
'm bšn't

§ 72b Hu.
ní-i-pa-wa/i (MALUS₂)*ha-ní-ia-ta-sa-tara/i-ti a-ta* |AEDIFICARE+*MI*¹-*ri+i* |*za-ia* "PORTA"-*la-na*

Ho.
[...*h*]*a*-[...]-*s*[*á*-...] *a*²-[*ta*] |AEDIFICARE+*MI*-[*ri+i*] |*za-ia* |"PORTA"-*la-na*

Phu/A III. 17–18
wbr' ys' hš'r z

§ 73 Hu.
wa/i-ta || ARHA |MANUS(-)*i-ti-tu* CAELUM (DEUS)TONITRUS-*hu-za-sá* CAELUM (DEUS)SOL-*za-sá* (DEUS)*i-ia-sá* OMNIS-*MI-zi-ha* DEUS-*ní-zi á-pa* |REX-*hi-sá* |*á-pa-há* "REX"-*na* |*á-pa-há-wa/i* |CAPUT-*ti-na*

Ho.
|*wa/i-ta* |ARHA |"*69"(-)*i-ti-tu* (DEUS)*i-ia-sá* |"CAELUM"(DEUS)TONITRUS-*hu-za-sá-'* |"CAELUM" (DEUS)SOL-‹*za*›-*sá* |OMNIS-*MI-zi-há-wa/i* DEUS-*ní-zi* |*á-pa-sá* REX-*ta-hi-sa* |*á-pa-há-'* |REX-*ti-na* |*á-pa-há-wa/i* CAPUT-*ti-na*

Phu/A III. 18–Phu/A IV. 1
wmḥ b'l šmm w'l qn 'rṣ wšmš 'lm wkl dr bn 'lm 'yt hmmlkt h' w'yt hmlk h' w'yt 'dm h' 'š 'dm šm

§ 74 Hu.
POST-*na-wa/i* ARHA?! ("CRUS<'>")*ta-za-tu* |*ara/i-zi* OMNIS-*MI-zi* (OCULUS)*á-za-ti-wa/i-tà-sa* |*á-ta₅/i₅-ma-za*

Ho.
POST-*na-ha-wa/i ara/i-*‹*zi*›-*i* |OMNIS-*MI-zi* |CRUS[...?]-*tu* [...

Phu/A IV. 1–2
'ps šm 'ztwd ykn l'lm

§ 75　　　Hu.
(DEUS)LUNA+*MI-sa-wa/i* (DEUS)SOL-*ha* REL-*ri+i*
á-ta₄/i₄-ma-za "CRUS"-*i*

Ho.
[—]

Phu/A IV. 2–3
km šm šmš wyrḥ

§§ 1–10　I am Azatiwadas, the Sun God's man,[7] servant of Tarhunzas,[8] whom Awarikus, king of Adanawa, made great. Tarhunzas made me mother and father to Adanawa,[9] and I caused Adanawa to prosper. I extended the plain of Adanawa on the one hand towards the west and on the other hand towards the east, and in my days Adanawa had all good things, plentiness, and luxury. I filled the Paharean granaries, and I made horse upon horse, and I made army upon army, and I made shield upon shield, all with (the help of) Tarhunzas and the gods.[10]

§§ 11–18　Thus I broke up the proud, and the evils which were inside the land, I moved them out of the land. And I benefitted the house of my lord, and I did all good things for the family of my lord. I caused them to sit on their father's throne.[11] And every king made me his father because of my justice and wisdom and goodness.[12]

---

7. For the title (DEUS)SOL-*mi-sá* CAPUT-*ti-i-sá*, /*tiwadamis zidis*/, Phoen. *hbrk bʻl*, see Goedegebuure in the forthcoming acts of the RAI 54, Würzburg, who argues that the title denotes an administrative function, "steward of the king."

8. The Storm God Tarhunzas is the head of the Luwian pantheon, equated here with Phoenician Baal.

9. The Luwian name lives on in the modern city Adana. Also note the very visual image created by this phrase, which recurs in the ÇİNEKÖY inscription. Azatiwadas appears as the city's benefactor, treating it kindly like a parent would treat its child.

10. The sentences explaining how Azatiwadas caused Adanawa to prosper are highly structured. The parallelism of Adanawa's extension to two sides is followed by a group of three nouns, describing the wealth of the city, yet all three seem to be paraphrases of the same idea. In particular, contrast the tripartite phrase "I made ..." with the shorter version occurring in the following (chronologically earlier) text, ÇİNEKÖY.

11. The Phoenician copy differs: "and I established peace with every king."

12. This is a standard phrase showing the ruler's good qualities—again, a pleasing group of three, or tricolon.

§§ 19-24 And I built strong fortresses on the frontiers, wherein bad men were: robbers, who had not fought(?)[13] under the house of Muksas.[14] And I, Azatiwadas, put them under my feet, and in those places I built fortresses so that Adanawa should dwell peacefully.[15]

§§ 25-31 And I smote strong fortresses towards the west, which former kings had not smitten, who were before me. But I, Azatiwadas, smote them, and I brought them down, and on my frontiers towards the east I made them settle down.[16] Thus I made Adanaweans settle down there.[17]

§§ 32-37 In my days, I extended the Adanawean frontiers, on the one hand towards the west and on the other hand towards the east, and even in those places which formerly were feared, where a man fears to walk the road, so in my days even women walk with spindles.[18] In my days, there was plentiness and luxury and good living, and Adanawa and the Adanawean plain dwelt peacefully.[19]

---

13. The Phoenician text has 'š bl 'š 'bd kn l-bt mpš, "none of whom had been servant to the house of MPŠ." The Luwian PUGNUS.PUGNUS-ta_4/i_4-, meanwhile, seems to necessitate a meaning "beat, fight."

14. Luwian Muksas, Phoenician MPŠ may be early attestations of a name well-known from Greek legend, Mopsus (Μόψος), founder of several cities in Pamphylia and Cilicia. Whether Luwian Muksas is the historical figure behind the legendary Mopsus, or a homonymous forefather is unknown but it seems likely that these traditions relate to one another.

15. Note the variation in the repetition of the phrase "I built fortresses"; the first attestation qualifies the fortresses as strong, the second omits this epithet but further specifies their *raison d'être*, namely, to protect Adanawa's peace.

16. The concept of fortresses continues, this time strong enemy fortresses. The emphasis here is on the fact that Azatiwadas smote them, a feat contrasted with the lack of such achievement by prior rulers, a standard comparison used to highlight one's own grandeur. The second affirmation "I smote them" repeats the verb for a third time in just a few clauses.

17. The newly conquered territory is thus secured by two means: deporting the native population to a different place and settling the territory with one's own people.

18. Followed by an allegorical metaphor, the vivid image of women peacefully strolling about. The spindle also appears as a symbol of womanhood.

19. Apart from repeating the phrase /amiyanza haliyanza/ "in my days" verbatim, this paragraph owes much to §§ 5-6 and 24, but on closer inspection one notes variation among the repetition, e.g., exchanging the plain of Adanawa for fortresses, "all good things" for "good living," the latter also in a different position within the tricolon.

§§ 38–44 I built this fortress, and I named it Azatiwadaya. So Tarhunzas and Runtiyas[20] were after me to build this fortress, and I built it [with (the help of) Tarhunzas ...] in my days [...[21]].

§§ 45–48 And I built [this] fortress,[22] and therein I made Tarhunzas [...] dwell. And every river land will begin to honor him (with) one ox a year, and a sheep at the time of harvesting and a sheep at the time of wine-making.[23]

§§ 49–59 Let him bless Azatiwadas with health and life, and let him be elevated above all kings. May the much blessed Tarhunzas and the gods of this fortress give to him, Azatiwadas, long days and many years and good abundance,[24] and let them give him victory over all kings. Thus let this fortress become (the home) of the Grain-God and the Wine-God.[25] And so the nations which dwell in (it) / which he shall make dwell in (it),[26] let them have sheep, oxen, food, and wine.[27] Much let them beget for us, and much let them make great for us, and much let them be in service to Azatiwadas and the house of Muksas with (the help of) Tarhunzas and the gods.[28]

§§ 60–75 If anyone from the kings, or (if) he (is) a man,[29] and he has a manly name, speaks this: "I shall delete the name of Azatiwadas from these gates here, and I shall carve in my name," or (if) he desires this fortress, and blocks up these gates,[30] which Azatiwadas made, and speaks thus: "I shall make these gates mine, and I shall write my own

---

20. Runtiyas or Runzas, the Stag God, is equated with Rešeph-of-the-goats in the Phoenician copy, presumably as god of the wild beasts.

21. The Phoenician copy fills the gap: "and I built it by the grace of Baal and by the grace of Rešeph-of-the-goats, in plenty and in luxury and in good living and in peace of heart, for it to be a protection for the plain of 'DN and for the house of MPŠ, since in my days there was plenty and luxury to the land of the plain of 'DN. And there was not in my days ever night(?) for the DNNYM."

22. The Phoenician has "established its name 'ZTWDY."

23. Following a standard pattern, the text ends with ritual obligations, blessings, and curses.

24. To create another tricolon, the verb is repeated before introducing, emphatically, a fourth object.

25. An allegorical expression for "let there always be enough to eat and drink."

26. Slightly differing versions in Hu. and Ho.

27. This translation paraphrases an awkward, more literal "let them become (those) of sheep, oxen, the Grain-God and the Wine-God."

28. This tricolon repeats the same initial word, the adverb man, "much," a scheme called anaphora.

29. The Phoenician has "prince."

30. Lit. "build in."

name (on them)." Or (if) from desire he shall block them up, or from badness or from evil he shall block up these gates, may celestial Tarhunzas, the celestial Sun, Ea[31] and all the gods delete that kingdom and that king and that man![32] In future, may Azatiwadas' name continue to stand for all ages, as the name of the Moon and of the Sun stands!

2.1.2. ÇİNEKÖY

This text of Warikas, king of Adana, is a much shorter inscription with only the first twelve clauses surviving. It antedates KARATEPE, and interestingly seems to have served as a model for the later text, using the same figures of speech albeit in a less elaborate way. Like KARATEPE, it is a Luwian-Phoenician bilingual, but its two language versions diverge further from one another. The text is carved onto the base of a massive Storm-God statue that was found on 30.10.1997 by O. Kadir Özer in Çineköy, ca. 30 km south of Adana. Since 5.4.1998, it has been on display in the Adana Museum. The statue base shows an ox-drawn cart, and the hieroglyphic text is written in between the animals' feet, on the back of the cart and partly on surface and side of the base. The character of the script resembles that of KARATEPE. The Phoenician text is written on the front piece of the base in between the oxen; preserved are eighteen lines. As for KARATEPE, dating rests on the possible identification of Warikas with Urikki of Que, who is attested for the years 738, 732, and 710–709 B.C.E.

The inscription records the deeds of Warikas of the house of Muksas. Firstly, the author identifies himself, and sums up his greatest deeds. He claims preferment by the gods, states his armament and his position of strength in relation to Assur and Hiyawa. He claims military successes, and then the text breaks off, presumably with more accounts of Warikas' good deeds. Despite the aforementioned parallels with KARATEPE, some of the readings and interpretations of this inscription remain quite unclear and uncertain.

§ 1 [EGO-*mi*] *wa/i+ra/i-i-*[*ka-sá* x-x-x-x(-x) ("INFANS")*ni-*]*mu-wa/i-za-sa* [*mu-ka*]*-sa-*[*si*]*-sa* || |INFANS.NEPOS-*si-sà* |*hi-ia-wa/i*[*-ni*]

-*sá* [(URBS)] |REX-*ti-sa* |(DEUS)TONIT[RUS]-*hu-t*[*a-sa* SERVUS-*ta$_4$/i$_4$-sa* (DEUS)SOL-*mi-sa* CAPUT-*ti-i-sa*]

---

31. The Phoenician version equates Ea, the God of wisdom and creation, with El QN 'RṢ.

32. The text is strewn with groups of three: here, three individual gods are invoked, followed by the entirety of gods, to punish in anticlimatic sequence kingdom, king and man.

§ 2   [*á-wa/i-mu*] *wa/i+ra/i-i-ka-sá* "[MAN]US"?(-)*la-tara/i-ha* [*hi-ia-wa/i-na*(URBS)]

§ 3   [*ARHA-ha-wa/i la+ra/i-a-nú-ha hi-*]*ia-wa/i-za*(URBS) *TERRA+LA+LA-za* || |(DEUS)TONITRUS-*hu-ta-ti* |*á-mi-ia-ti-ha* |*tá-ti-ia-ti* |DEUS-*na*<-*ti*>

§ 4 |*wa/i-ta* (EQUUS.ANIMAL)*zú-na* (EQUUS)*zú-wa/i* |SUPER+*ra/i-ta* |*i-zi-ia-ha*

§ 5   EXER[CITUS-*la/i/u-za-ha*] (||) EXERCITUS[-*la/i/u-ni*] |SUPER+*ra/i-ta* |*i-z*[*i*]-*ia-h*[*a*]

§ 6 |REL-*p*[*a*]-*wa/i-mu-u* |*su+ra/i-wa/i-ni-sa*(URBS) |REX-*ti-sá* |*su+ra/i-wa/i-za-ha*(URBS) |DOMUS-*na-za* |*ta-ni-ma-za* |*tá-*[*ti-sa* MATER-*sa-ha*] (||) *i-zi-ia-si*

§ 7 |*hi-ia-wa/i-sa-ha-wa/i*(URBS) |*su+ra/i-ia-sa-ha*(URBS) |"UNUS"-*za* |DOMUS-*na-za* |*i-zi-ia-si*

§ 8   REL-*pa-wa/i* ||*274-*[*ta*]-*li-ha* (CASTRUM)*ha+ra/i-na-sà* [PUGNUS(-)*la/i/u-mi-tà-ia-sà*]

§ 9   AEDIFICARE-*MI-ha-ha-wa/i*] |ORIENS-*mi-ia-ti* |*la-i*[*a*]-*ni* 8 || OCCIDENS-*mi-ti-ha* 7 CASTRUM-*za*

§ 10 |REL-*pa-wa/i* ("LOCUS")*pi$_x$-tà-za* |*za-ia* "FLUMEN"-*sa pa+ra/i-ni-wa/i-zi* (||) |MAGNUS+*ra/i* *180.*311-*za* |*á-sa-tá*

§ 11 || *wa/i-a* |*á-mu* |*a-mi-ia-ti* COR-*na-ti* || ("TERRA")*ta-sà*-REL+*ra/i* REL$^?$/*zi*$^?$ || |*i*$^?$-*zi*$^?$-*ia-*[*x*$^?$](-)*á*$^?$-*wa/i* URBS-*MI*$^?$-*ni-zi* SOLIUM$^?$ [   ] | || [

§ 12 OMNIS-*MI-ma*$^?$]-*ia* ARHA (BONUS)*u-sa-nu-mi-na*

Phoenician (based on Lemaire 2000)

1. 'nk w[r(y)k bn ....?
2. 'špḥ mpš [mlk dnnym?]
3. hbrk b'l 'š [yrḥbt]
4. bt 'rṣ 'mq ['dn b'br]
5. b'l wb'rr ' [lm wp']
6. l 'nk 'p ss ['l ss (w)m]
7. ḥnt 'l mḥnt wmlk ['šr w]
8. kl bt 'šr kn ly l'b [wl]
9. 'm wdnnym w'šrym
10. kn lbt 'ḥdwbn 'nk ḥmy[t]

11. bmṣ' šmš šmnt 8 wbm
12. b' šmš šb't 7 wkn 15
13. wbmq[m ...] šwrk/b
14. k/p [...] ' [...]b/ḥ [...]
15. myt wyr [...]h/rt
16. 'ṣm/n yšbt š[m ...]k/n b'l
17. kr štq yš' šb' w[kl]n'm
18. 'l mlk h' w'p bn/m[ ]l[...]nh'

§§ 1–12 [I am] Wari[kas],[33] so[n of ..., Muk]sas's grandson, King of the Hiyawaeans,[34] Tarhun[za's servant, the Sun God's man. And I,] Warikas, extended [Hiyawa. And] I caused the plain of Hiyawa to prosper because of Tarhunza and my paternal gods. And I made horse upon horse, and I made ar[my] upon ar[my]. And so the king of the Assyrians[35] and the entire house of Assur became fa[ther and mother] to me.[36] And Hiyawa and Assur became one house. Indeed I smote strong fortresses(?). [And I built] towards the east 8, towards the west 7 fortresses.[37] ... And I through my person made lands ... For al]l to be made very good(?) [...

---

33. The loss of the kings' initial *a*- may be explained as aphaeresis, a process apparently attested in other names. But why he should be Awarikus in KARATEPE and (A) warikas in this text, is still unexplained. The two hieroglyphic symbols for *ka* and *ku* are not alike in shape, and clearly represent two different vowels.

34. The ÇİNEKÖY inscription does not use the narrower term *Adanawa*-, which refers to the capital city, but the wider term *Hiyawa*-, which refers to the Cilician plain, if not beyond. Note that the Phoenician versions of both inscriptions use the term 'DNNYM. The connection *Hiyawa*- = *Hyp-akhaioi* = *Aḫḫiyawa* remains to be proven.

35. On the problem of the Luwian toponym *sura*-, see most recently Simon, forthcoming. For this inscription, the identification with Assur is assured by the Phoenician text version.

36. Compare how in KARATEPE the Storm God, Tarhunzas, made Azatiwadas "mother and father of Adanawa." It is unlikely, however, that this signifies a change from vassal status to a more independent position. The ÇİNEKÖY inscription of Awarikus reflects the position of Urikki, who is mentioned as tributary king of Que (Cilicia Pedias) for the years 738 and 732 B.C.E. in the Assyrian annals; yet it remains uncertain whether the two are identical or merely homonymous. If Azatiwadas is correctly identified as Sanduarri, king of Kundi (classical Kyinda, presumably modern Anavarza) and Sissu (classical Sisium, modern Kozan), whom the Assyrian king Esarhaddon had killed in 676 B.C.E., then his omission to refer to Assyrian rule in Cilicia may have been part of his rebellious actions that brought about his downfall.

37. Compare how this plain statement of fact—if restored correctly—is turned into eloquent literary phrases in Azatiwadas's inscription.

2.2. FUNERARY AND COMMEMORATIVE INSCRIPTIONS

Inscribed stelae were set up by kings and private individuals alike to mark the passing of a person and commemorate him or her. Given that the execution of such a stone monument would have involved a high degree of skill and therefore cost, we must assume that this practice remained the privilege of society's higher ranking people. Indeed, longer commemorative inscriptions, such as TOPADA and MARAŞ 1, are invariably memorials to rulers.

The following selection of funerary and commemorative inscriptions illustrates the range of this genre, from one-sentence statements recalling name and existence of a person, not unlike our modern convention of inscribing name and dates of birth and death on a gravestone, to providing some or much further information. For instance, we may hear about the family of the deceased, especially his or her children, who are frequently named as having commissioned the monument. Likewise, a eulogy on the deceased might be included, such as the life of Ruwas (KULULU 4). Alternatively, obligations might be imposed on surviving family members, and gods tend to be invoked to protect the monument. Sadly, these texts offer almost no insight into the religious significance of death, the references to deities being no different in this to any other genre recorded in Hieroglyphic Luwian.

2.2.1. TİLSEVET

Most funerary inscriptions are relatively short, like this inscription of Uwawas. The text is inscribed on a stele discovered by a villager in an ancient graveyard outside the village of Tilsevet, ca. 35 km southeast of Gaziantep; as the archaeological context of its discovery could not be established, it is uncertain whether it was found *in situ*. The stele was added to the Gaziantep museum collection in 1955. It can be dated to the eighth century B.C.E.

The inscription uses similar clauses as several other funerary texts from Karkamiš, which suggests that these are the stock phrases appropriate to this kind of monument.

1 § 1   *za-wa/i* (STELE)*wa/i-ni-zi*¹ *u-wa/i-wa/i-sa ta-ta*

  § 2   FEMINA-*ti-zi-wa/i-mu-ta á-mi-zi ara/i-zi ha-si-ha*

  § 3   *a-wa/i* |*462 *77-*ha* ||

2 § 4   FEMINA.*462-*ti-pa-wa/i* DARE-*ha*

	§ 5	wa/i-mu-u |za ("STELE")wa/i-ni-za á-mi-zi INFANS.NI-zi BONUS-sa-tà-ti CRUS-nu-ta||
3	§ 6	za-ti-pa-wa/i (STELE)wa/i-ni-ri+i REL-sà ("CORNU")tara/i-pi-wa/i CRUS-i
	§ 7	wa/i-tu-u DEUS-ni-zi LIS-za-tu-u

§§ 1–7   This stele was erected as Uwawas's. I enjoyed my womanly times fully.[38] I pledged (male) issue but I gave female issue. This stele my children erected for me in goodness. Who(soever) tramples on this stele,[39] may the gods litigate against him!

2.2.2. KARKAMIŠ A1b

The following text, a funerary dedication, comes from the city of Karkamiš. The inscription A1b was carved into an orthostat that belonged to the Long Wall of Sculpture. It carries a dedication by the wife of the tenth-century B.C.E. ruler Suhis II. Her name is recorded in mixed logographic-phonetic writing as BONUS-*tis*. We do not know the name behind this spelling, as the logogram BONUS is used to represent several words meaning "good."

Suhis erected the Long Wall of Sculpture at Karkamiš, and one may assume that this monument with its inscription was set up after the death of his wife. The text is accompanied by a picture of a seated female figure, presumably BONUS-*tis*, who holds a spindle and raises her left arm in the posture assumed by the hieroglyphic sign for "I," EGO, that is, pointing to her face with her hand. She is flanked by a nude, winged goddess on her right. The text differs from other commemorative inscriptions: the deceased lady demands that her husband keep the memory of her name alive with his; such a stipulation is, of course, pertinent when applied to a ruler who would leave further inscriptions but would make little sense among private individuals.

1	§ 1	EGO-mi-i ^IBONUS-ti-sa ^Isu-hi-si-i REGIO-ní(-)DOMINUS-ia-i-sa |BONUS-mi-sa || FEMINA-ti-i-sa
2		
	§ 2	wa/i-ti-*a mi-i-sa-*a VIR-ti-i-sa REL-i-ta REL-i-ta ||
3		|á-ta$_5$/i$_5$-ma-za i-zi-i-sa-ta-i

---

38. For the verb *hasi*- "enjoy to the full," see Melchert 2004b: 376.
39. For a recent discussion of the verb *tarpi*- see Yakubovich 2002.

§ 3 |mu-pa-wa/i-ta-*a || |BONUS-sa₅+ra/i-ti CUM-ní i-zi-i-sa-ta-i

§§ 1–3 I (am) BONUS-tis, the dear wife of the Country-Lord Suhis. Wheresoever my husband honors his own name, he shall also honor me with goodness.

2.2.3. KARKAMIŠ A5b

The following short inscription belongs to a group of funerary inscriptions found at Karkamiš, dating to the eighth century B.C.E. and resembling one another. This short text was written on a stele which was reused as a tombstone in Roman times. It remembers an otherwise unknown individual called Nunuras.

1 § 1 EGO?-(m)u? nu-nu+ra/i-sá (DIES)ha-li (PES₂)pa-za-ha||
2 § 2 ara/i-zi-pa-mu!-ta ha-si-ha

§§ 1–2 I, Nunuras, passed (my) days, and I enjoyed (my) times to the full.

2.2.4. MEHARDE, SHEIZAR

This pair of stelae comes from the Hama region. The MEHARDE stele shows the figure of a woman, holding up two unidentified objects of conical shape. To her left is another small figure in long dress, facing right. Both are standing on a reclining lion. The inscription is placed on all four sides of the stele, taking up all of the two narrow sides and a limited amount of space on the two wider sides, including the space under the sculpted picture. As the text carries a dedication to a goddess, one may wonder whether the female figure depicted might be said "divine Queen of the Land," who is invoked in only one other Luwian inscription. The text was commissioned by Taitas, king of Watasatina.

The second stele, SHEIZAR, carries the funerary inscription of Taitas's wife, Kupapiyas, and one may therefore assume that MEHARDE was the funerary stele of Taitas. Since both Taitas and Kupapiyas invoke the "divine Queen of the Land," she may either have been a personal goddess, possibly Kubaba,[40] or the appropriate authority as a goddess of the underworld. The dating of both stelae is problematic, as it is uncertain whether the script is archaic or archaizing. It falls into the period of ca. 900–700 B.C.E.

---

40. Melchert (pers. comm.) points out that this possibility is supported by the fact that Kupapiyas, lit. "Kubaba gave (her)," is named after this deity.

(MEHARDE)

A1 § 1 |za-a-wa/i |(STELE)ta-ni?-||sà-za |DEUS.REGIO-ni-sa ||
|(MAGNUS.DOMINA)ha-su-sa₅+ra/i-sa ||

§ 2 |i-zi-i-tà-pa-wa/i-tú ta||-i-ta-sa |HEROS||-li-sa |wa/i-ta₄/i₄-sà-||ti-ni-za-sa(REGIO) || ‹REX-ti?›-sa

§ 3 [|a]-wa/i || |za-a-ti |(STELE)ta||-ni-si |REL-i-sà ||[…

B1 § 4 …]zi x x |za-a-si-na x x x(-)za-´ |REL?-a?-ha || |FORTIS-si-i?

§ 5 |PUGNUS(-)wa/i+ra/i-ma-a-ti-pa-wa/i-t[i?] […]

C1 REL-i-sà

§ 6 |pa-ti-*a||-pa-wa/i |DEUS.REGIO-||ni-si |(MAGNUS.DOMINA)ha-su-||sa₅+ra/i-sa |LIS-za-||sa-li-sà |sá-tú-*a

§ 7 || |z[a]-pa-[wa/i] |(STELE)||ta-ni-sà-za || |REL-i-sa |LOCUS-ta₄/i₄-||za |SA₄-ni-ti

D1 § 8 |pa-sa-pa-wa/i x-x-x-za |DEUS.REGIO-||ni-si |(MAGNUS.DOMINA)ha-su-sa₅+ra/i-sa |ARHA |DELERE-nu-tú

§ 9 || |CAPERE+MALLEUS ¹á-SCALPRUM-za-sa |BONUS₂. SCRIBA-la/i/u-sa

(SHEIZAR)

1 § 1 EGO-wa/i-mi ku-pa-pi-ia-sa ¹ta-i-ta-si FEMINA-na-tí-sa HEROS-sa wa/i- ta₄/i₄-sà-ti-[ni-s]i(REGIO)

2 § 2 |wa/i-*a |mi-ia+ra/i||-*a |(IUSTITIA)tara/i-wa/i-na-ti |CENTUM-ni |ANNUS-si-na |(PES₂)pa-za-ha_x

§ 3 |wa/i-mu-ta-*a |mi-zi-*a |INFANS-ni-zi |"LONGUS"-zi |FLAMMAE(?)(-)ha_x||-si |PONERE?-wa/i-ta

3

§ 4 |za-pa-wa/i-mu |(STELE)ta-‹ni›-sà |mi-i-zi-*a|INFANS.NEPOS-zi |INFANS.NEPOS-ka-la-zi |(INFANS)NEG₂-wa/i-zi || x-x(-)za-wa/i-nu-wa/i-ta

4

§ 5 á?-mi-wa/i-tá |wa/i-[…]-´ |mi-sa-*a |REL-i-sa |INFANS.NEPOS-si-sa |INFANS.NEPOS||-ka-la-[sa] |(INFANS)NEG₂-wa/i-sa |(INFANS)NEG₂-‹wa/i›-[NEG₂-]wa/i-sa […

5

§ 6 [RE]L-s[a? …]-i

6	§ 7		pa-ti-[pa]-wa/i-*a		DEUS.REGIO-ni-si-i (DOMINA)ha-su-sa₅+ra/i-sa	LIS	-li-sa	sa-tu-*a
7	§ 8	MALLEUS.CAPERE-pa-wa/i-na ¹LOCUS-ti		-*273-wa/i-sa BONUS₂.SCRIBA-la-sa
	§ 9	SERVUS-ta₅/i₅-sa-pa-wa/i-tu(-)mi [...]-sa pa+ra/i-na x-x

MEHARDE

§§ 1-2   This stele (belongs to) the divine Queen of the Land. The hero Taitas, king of Walistin,[41] made (it) for her.

§§ 3-8   And who(ever) [...] to this stele, ⌈...⌉. But who(ever) shall [...] for himself, the divine Queen of the Land shall be his prosecutor! And who(ever) shall overturn this stele in (its) place, may the divine Queen of the Land destroy his ...![42]

§ 9   A-*268-zas,[43] the Good(?)[44] Scribe, carved (this).

SHEIZAR

§§ 1-4   I am Kupapiyas, wife of the hero Taitas, king of Walistin. Because of my justice, I lived a hundred years. And my children put(?) me on the

---

41. Reading the sign ta_4/i_4 with its /l/ value leads to a country Walistin, recently also attested in a new inscription by a (homonymous?) king Taitas as *Palistin*, "Palestine." Hawkins (2011: 51; 53) argues that a linguistic connection of Luwian palistin with "Philistine" is possible, and views the alternation of Luwian p/w as differing reflections of f. Current evidence suggests that this country had its center at Tell Tayinat in the Amuq plain, included Aleppo and Ain Dara, and later possibly extended to Karkamiś and, attested here, to Meharde-Sheizar.

42. A typical phrase would be "destroy his name" but the remaining traces do not seem to fit here.

43. The name is written *á*-SCALPRUM-*za-sa*. The phonetic value of the logographic sign *268, SCALPRUM, remains unknown. However, the sign is connected with the act of writing, as it presumably depicts a chisel, the tool used to engrave writing on stone. It would not be surprising if the scribe's name contained a reference to the highly exclusive skill of his trade (most likely a family trade), either as a linguistic element, if the sign is to be interpreted as a logogram or, if it were used here with a phonetic value, the scribe may have invented a playful way of writing his own name.

44. It remains uncertain whether we should understand "Good Scribe" as a title denoting rank, that is, a highly skilled scribe. The same element occurs on seals, where one may reasonably interpret it as a blessings formula, that is, "good (things) to the scribe," but such a formula would be unorthodox within a literary text.

	... pyre(?),[45] and my grandchildren, great-grandchildren (and) great-great-grandchildren caused this stele to ...[46]
§§ 5–7	And among my [posterity?], who(ever is) my grandchild, great-grandchild, great-great-grandchild, great-great-great-grandchild: who(soever) shall [harm them?], the divine Queen of the Land shall be his prosecutor!
§§ 8–9	Pedantimuwas, the Good(?) Scribe, carved it, and (as) servant to him [...[47] (was?)] present(?).[48]

2.2.5. KULULU 4

The funerary inscription of the Tabalean ruler Ruwas is singular in that it is a posthumous royal inscription, datable to ca. 750–740 B.C.E. The four-sided stele carries two separate texts, a longer, first-person narrative in which the author reviews his life and in particular, his good deeds, and a short, one-sentence inscription by his nephew, Hulis, stating that he erected this monument.

1	§ 1	EGO-wa/i-mi ru-wa/i-sa$_4$ IUDEX-ní-sa á-sá-ha SOL-wa/i+ra/i-mi-sa$_8$
	§ 2	NEPOS-ta-ha-wa/i-mu SOL-wa/i+ra/i-mi-sa$_8$
	§ 3	AQUILA-wa/i-mu DEUS-ni-i-zi (LITUUS)á-za-ta
	§ 4	wa/i-mu-ta (LITUUS)á-za-mi-na COR-tara/i-na a-ta tu-tá
2	§ 5	|a-wa/i á-mi-ia-za || DOMINUS-na-za ¹IUDEX-la COR-la-ti-i-´ SUB-na-na SARMA+RA/I+MI-ia-za-ha
	§ 6	wa/i-ta DOMINUS-na-za-´ á-mi-ia-za BONUS-si-ia-za-ha
	§ 7	|wa/i-mu LEPUS+ra/i-ia-la-ta
	§ 8	DOMINUS-ni-ha-wa/i-mu DOMUS-ní-i DOMUS-ni(-)DOMINUS-ni-i-sa$_4$ |á-sá-ha
3	§ 9	wa/i-mu-ta DEUS-ni-zi-i (LITUUS)á-za-mi-na || COR-ni-na a-ta tu-wa/i-mi-na-´ la-ta |wa/i-li?-ia-wa/i-ti-na

---

45. Could this rather unclear sentence refer to cremation as a funerary practice?
46. Be erected? The first few signs of the verb are illegible because of damage.
47. The name of the assistant scribe is missing.
48. Given that very few Luwian inscriptions even mention the name of their scribe, it is fascinating that this text seems to include not just the responsible scribe but his assistant, too.

§ 10 |wa/i-ta á-mi-zi-i DOMINUS-ni-zi |wa/i-su u-sa₄-nú-wa/i-ha

§ 11 OMNIS-ma-si-sa₄-ha-wa/i-mi tá-ti-sa₄ á-sa₈-ha

§ 12 a-wa/i OMNIS-mi sa-na-wa/i-sa₈ CUM-ní i-zi-i-sa-ta-ha

4 § 13 |á-mi-sa||-ha-wa/i-‹mu› |*274-ti-sa x-la-x-i |x [...

§ 14 |‹á›-mi-[ia-za]-ha-[wa/i ...] |u-‹si›-na-s‹a›-za |ha+ra/i-[...

top

§ 15 |za-wa/i STELE ¹hu-li-sa₄ |PONERE-ta ¹ru-wa/i-sa₈ |FRATER.LA-sa₈ |INFANS-ni-sa₈

§ 16 PRAE-sa₈-pa-wa/i || "*476"(-)TERRA-li-ia-ta

§§ 1–14 I was the ruler Ruwas,⁴⁹ the Sun God's man⁵⁰ and my posterity belongs to the Sun God. The gods loved my times, and they put into me a beloved soul. And I ...ed under my lords (and) Labarna⁵¹ with my soul. And I was dear(?) to my lords, and they made me governor(?), and in the lord's house I was house-lord. And the gods received the beloved soul which was put in(side), raised(?).⁵² And I blessed my lords well, and I was every man's father, and I honored the good for every man. And for me my ... [...]. And for my eunuchs ... [...].⁵³

49. If correctly identified, Ruwas is the author of another Luwian inscription, KULULU 1, where he identifies himself as Ruwas, servant of Tuwatis. This provides a date for these inscriptions, ca. 740–730 B.C.E., the time of Tuwatis's rule. Another hieroglyphic inscription, TOPADA (p. 54), identifies Tuwatis as the father of the ruler Wasusarma, who features in Assyrian annals as Wassurme.

50. See Goedegebuure in the forthcoming acts of the 54th RAI, Würzburg.

51. Labarna, the name of the first Hittite king, became a royal title, written with the hieroglyphs IUDEX+la, just like the name of Caesar became a dynastic title. As a title, it is almost exclusively confined to the Bronze Age, and here it is clearly marked with the hieroglyph for personal names, therefore presumably signifying a name rather than a title. The content seems to imply that "my lords and Labarna" where figures of authority, of higher rank than Ruwas himself. To find such a person by this name some 450 years after the title was last used by a Hittite king, is certainly noteworthy. An alternative interpretation could render a name Tarwanalas, as the logogram IUDEX is used to write the word *tarwani-*, "ruler."

52. The soul is placed into a person at birth and reverts back to the gods when he dies. Does it literally *rise up* to the gods?

53. The last two sentences of Ruwas's statement are not well enough preserved to be translated fully. Might one expect here honors conferred upon or obligations under-

§§ 15–16 This stele Hulis, Ruwas's brother's child, placed. And he ... .

2.2.6. MARAŞ 1

Hieroglyphic inscriptions survive on different types of stone monuments, ranging from square building blocks to rock reliefs, via free-standing stelae and ornamentally carved pieces of stone masonry. The portal lion from the citadel gate of Maraş falls into the latter category. It was discovered in the late nineteenth century C.E. in an important Iron Age city, the capital of the Neo-Hittite state Gurgum. The following inscription is carved onto the lion's body and may have continued on a further building block, however, this is not preserved and the surviving text is incomplete, breaking off after twelve clauses. It commemorates Halparuntiyas III, king of Gurgum/Maraş (ninth century B.C.E.). The surviving text does not settle the question whether the author was already deceased at the time when the inscription was made. Its most interesting feature is an exceedingly long genealogy; linguistically, this is an important passage because of the many relationship terms it contains. The text preserved after the extensive introduction of the royal author uses a succession of stock phrases known from a variety of other Luwian inscriptions. It is unfortunate that only a part of the text is preserved, and we therefore cannot know whether the entire inscription was composed in this manner. One peculiarity of this text is that it seems to use the vowel sign *209, i, to mark the end of words. This is a rare practice of very few inscriptions only.

1	§ 1 a	EGO-wa/i-mi-i ᴵTONITRUS.*HALPA-pa-ru-ti-i-ia-sa* |("IUDEX")*tara/i-wa/i-ni-sà* |*ku+ra/i-ku-ma-wa/i-ni-i-sà*(URBS) REX-*ti-i-sa*
	b	ᴵ*la+ra/i+a-ma-si-i-sa* |LEPUS+*ra/i-ia-li-i-sa* |INFANS-*mu-wa/i-za-sá*
2	c	ᴵTONITRUS.*HALPA-pa-ru-ti-ia-si-sà* || HEROS-*li-sa* |(INFANS.NEPOS)*ha-ma-si-sá-'*
	d	*mu-wa/i-ta-li-si-sà* |("SCALPRUM+RA/I.LA/I/U")*wa/i+ra/i-pa-li-sa* |(INFANS.NEPOS)*ha-ma-su-ka-la-sá*
	e	ᴵTONITRUS.*HALPA-pa*-CERVUS$_2$-*ti-ia-si-sà*
3		|("IUDEX")*tara/i-wa/i-ni-sá* || |(INFANS)*na-wa/i-sa*
	f	ᴵ*mu-wa/i-zi-si* HEROS-*li-sà* |(INFANS)*na-wa/i-na-wa/i-sá*

---

taken on behalf of the dead ruler by his ... and his eunuchs?

	g	¹*la+ra/i+a-ma-si-sá* LEPUS+*ra/i-ia-li-sa* |(INFANS)*ha+ra/i-tu-sá*
	h	DEUS-*na-ti* (LITUUS)*á-za-mi-sà* CAPUT-*ta-ti* ‹(LITUUS)›
4		*u-ni-mi-sa* |FINES-*ha-ti* ‖ AUDIRE-*mi-sà* REX-*ti-sá*
	i	(LITUUS)*á-za-mi-sa* |(BONUS)*u-li-ia-mi-sà* |("PANIS.SCU-TELLA")*mu-sa*?-*nu-wa/i-ti-sá* |("PANIS")*ma-li*-‹*ri+i*›-*mi-i-sá* REX-*ti-sá*
	§ 2	|*wa/i-mu* |*á-mi-i-zi* |*tá-ti-zi* DEUS-*ni-zi-i* |(LITUUS)*á-za-ta*
	§ 3	|*wa/i-mu-ta* |*á-mi* |*tá-ti-i* |(THRONUS)*i-sà-tara/i-ti-i* (SOLIUM)*i-sà-nu-wa/i-ta*
5	§ 4	|*a-wa/i* |("VACUUS")*ta-na-ta-*´("SOLIUM")*i-sa-*||*nu-wa/i-ha*
	§ 5	|"SOLIUM"(-)*x-ma-ma-pa-wa/i* BONUS(-)*u-su-tara/i-ha* (DEUS)TONITRUS-*hu-ta-sá-ti-i* (DEUS)*i-ia-sa-ti-ha* LEPUS+*ra/i-ia-ti*
	§ 6	|*wa/i-mu-ta* |LIS+*la/i/u-si-sá* (DEUS)[…]-*ti-i*?-*sá* |*i-mára/i-si-ha*-ⁱ (DEUS)*ru-ti-ia-sá*-ⁱ |("IUDEX")*tara/i-wa/i-na-za-ta-*´
	§ 7	|*wa/i-mu*¹ |("IUSTITIA")*tara/i-wa/i-na+ra/i* |*ha-pa*(-)x(-)*ha-la-i-ta*
	§ 8	|*wa/i-mu* |*za* |*273-pa-*x-x[… ‖
6	§ 9	[… …]-*ia-ha-*´ |"PES₂"(-)*ti-ri+i-*‹*ha*› |REL-*ta*
	§ 10	|*wa/i-mu* x x x |x-*tara/i-za*-ⁱ |PRAE-ⁱ |("CAPERE")*la-la-ta*
	§ 11	|*i-mára/i-si-pa-wa/i-mu*-ⁱ (DEUS)CERVUS₂-*ti-ia-sá* |REL-*za* «-*wa/i*?» |(BESTIA)HWI-*tara/i* |*pi-pa-sa-ta*
7	§ 12	|*wa/i-ta* ‖ |*á-mi-zi* |*tá-ti-zi* […

§ 1 I (am/was) Halparuntiyas, the ruler, Gurgumean king, son of Laramas the governor, grandson of the hero Halparuntiyas, great-grandson of the brave Muwatalis, great-great-grandson of the ruler Halparuntiyas, great-great-great-grandson of the hero Muwizis, descendant of the governor Laramas.

§§ 2–5 A king loved by the gods, known by the people, heard of abroad, a loved, exalted, satisfying(?), honey-sweet king.[54] My paternal gods

---

54. Note the symmetry of genealogy and royal epithets, which consist of seven elements each.

loved me, and they seated me on my father's throne. And I settled the devastated (places), and I benefited(?) the settlements(?) by the authority of Tarhunzas and Eas."[55]

§§ 6-12 The gods [...-]tis of the Lawsuit and Runtiyas of the Countryside made me ruler, and because of (my) justice they ...ed me, [...] where I ...ed, they brought [...] before me. But what(ever) wild beast Runtiyas of the Countryside(?) gave to me, my fathers [...[56]

2.2.7. TOPADA

This long, commemorative inscription was set up by or on behalf of the Tabalean ruler Wasusarmas, son of Tuwatis. The text was incised into a rock face near the village of Topada (now Açıgöl). The script shows archaizing features and uses a high number of unusual sign forms, most of which can only be elucidated from the context; some recur in inscriptions of relative temporal proximity, such as KULULU 4 (p. 50). Unusual signs are not the only difficulty of this inscription, rendering the reading of the text very uncertain.

A further noteworthy feature are the titles of the author. Wasusarmas calls himself 'Great King, Hero', titles which trace back to the Hittite Empire and may have been employed to create an archaic effect. The historical figure of Wasusarmas can be identified as Wassurme, attested in Assyrian annals for ca. 728-730 B.C.E., therefore providing an approximate date for the inscription. Its content, too, is uncommon. The text narrates political and military events, particularly cavalry engagements.

1	§ 1	[MAGNUS.]REX $wali_4$-su-SARMA-ma-sa ‹MAGNUS.›REX HEROS $tú$-$wali_4$-ti-sa_7 MAGNUS.REX HEROS-li-sa INFANS
	§ 2	$wali_4$-su-SARMA-ma-sa_7(-)$wali_5$ FORTIS-zi/a-ti PRAE-na X.PISCIS?(-)$sà$-ta_x
2	§ 3	$wali$-mu pa+$rali$-za_5-ta_x(URBS) 8 REX-ti-sa POST+$rali$-zi/a FRONS-$la/i/u$-zi/a-ha x[...?](-)‖sa-ta_x

---

55. These are standard topoi used to illustrate kingship, and the relationship between king and deities. See in this volume alone: the king loved by his gods (KULULU 4, MARAŞ 1, KARKAMIŠ A11a, KARKAMIŠ A6, TELL AHMAR 6 and TELL AHMAR 1); succession to paternal throne granted by the gods (KULULU 4, KARKAMIŠ A11a, KARKAMIŠ A2+3, MARAŞ 1, TELL AHMAR 6 and TELL AHMAR 1); resettlement of depopulated areas (KARATEPE 1, MARAŞ 1).

56. Presumably, this sentence would contrast Halparuntiyas' achievements, here success in hunting, with those of his predecessors, i.e., as many wild beasts as the stag god granted him (to shoot), he did not grant his fathers and grandfathers (cf. BOHÇA).

	§ 4	wa/i-mu tara/i-zi/a REX-ti-zi/a CUM-ni wa/i_6-sa_7-ta_x wa/i_5+ra/i-pa-la_x-wa/i-sa_x ki_x-ia-ki_x-ia-sa_4-ha ru-wa/i_7-ta_x-sa-ha *92
	§ 5	á-mu-$ha^?$/$pa^?$-wa/i REX+RA/I-ti (ANIMAL)EQUUS-wa/i-ti u-pa-ha
	§ 6	a-wa/i á-mí-i<<a>>-NEG_2 FINES+RA/I+HA-ha-lí CASTRUM-ni-sa_7 PONERE-wa/i-ha
3	§ 7	pa+ra/i-za_5-ta_x-$sí^?$-sa_6-‹x›-wa/i-mu-ta_x FINES+HI ‖ CURRUS(-)x-ta_x
	§ 8	wa/i-sa ("PES_2")i+ra/i á-pa-sa_5-ti (ANIMAL)EQUUS-wa/i-ti OMNIS-MI-ti EXERCITUS-la/i/u-ti-ha á-pa_x-$sí^?$-na FINES+RA/I+HI-NEG_2 zi/a-ara/i ta_x-ri+i-ta_x
	§ 9	PONERE-wa/i-ta_x-pa-wa/i-ta_x MONS-ti
	§ 10	á-mu-pa_x-wa/i_8-mi-ta_x a_x-mí-ia+ra/i REX+RA/I-ti (ANIMAL)EQUUS-wa/i-ti x-zá ANNUS(-)na-ha-sa_x-ha_x
	§ 11	a-wa/i 2-sú zi/a-sa_6-ta_5/i_5
	§ 12	CUM-ta_x-ta_x-pa-wa/i-mí-ta_x ANNUS(-)na-ha-sa_5-ha
	§ 13	wa/i-sa pa+ra/i-za_5-ta_x-wa/i-ni_x(URBS) "TERRA"-REL_x+ra/i *273-ti ("PES_2")i+ra/i
4	§ 14	wa/i_5-ta_x ‖ URBS+MI.AEDIFICIUM-ta_x-na FLAMMAE(?)(-)la_x-há-nú-wa/i-ta_x
	§ 15	*274-ia-pa-wa/i FEMINA.MANUS-zi/a-ha SERVUS-sa ("PES")u-pa-ta_x
	§ 16	MAGNUS+ra/i-zi/a-pa-wa/i-mu (ANIMAL)EQUUS-sa POST+ra/i(-$ti^?$) FINES+HI(-$ti^?$)-zi/a (LITUUS)ti-ia+ra/i-ta_x
	§ 17	wa/i-mu á-mí-sa_4 DOMINUS-ni-sa (DEUS)TONITRUS-zi/a-sa_8 (DEUS)SARMA-sa_8 (DEUS)*198-sa_6 (DEUS)BOS.*206.PANIS-sa_8-ha PRAE-na *179-ia-ta_x
	§ 18	wa/i-mi-ta_x tù-pa-sa_6-ti wa/i_5-sú-ha
	§ 19	a-mi-sa-há-wa/i_5-tú-ta_x REX+RA/I-sa_7 (ANIMAL)EQUUS-sa_4 FRONS-ti-ia-$sí^?$-sa FRONS-ti-sa_7 ANNUS-na 2-zi/a "TERRA"-REL+ra/i a-ta_x ‖ ta-x(URBS) *274(-)sà-ta_x
5	§ 20	wa/i_7-tù-´ ANNUS tara/i-zi/a TERRA-REL_x+ra/i ta-x(URBS) a-ta_x CRUS+FLUMEN-ta_x

§ 21 wa/i-tà 3 ANNUS MAGNUS-zi/a (ANIMAL)EQUUS-zi/a FRONS-ti(ras.)-ia-sa$_5$+ra/i FRONS-ti-ia+ra/i x-sí?(-)sa-ta$_x$

§ 22 wa/i-mu-ta$_x$ 3 LUNA+MI-zi/a x-pa-zi/a PRAE-na *273-pa-mi(-)NEG$_3$ ta$_x$-ta$_x$-‹tà?›

§ 23 zi/a-tà-pa-wa/i-ta$_x$ CRUS.CRUS (ANIMAL)EQUUS-ti pa+ra/i-za$_5$-ta$_x$-wa/i-ni(URBS) "TERRA"-REL+ra/i INFRA?-ta$_x$-ta$_x$ ("PES$_2$")pa-zi/a-ta$_x$||

§ 24 [...]URBS [FLAMMAE(?)?](-)la$_x$-ha-nú-wa/i-ta$_x$

§ 25 *74-wa/i$_7$-sà-pa-wa/i REL$_x$+RA/I-ta$_x$ *274 FEMINA.MANUS-ha SERVUS-wa/i ARHA? u-pa-‹ta$_x$›

§ 26 pa+ra/i-za$_5$-ta$_x$-wa/i$_9$-ni-sa-pa-wa/i-ta$_x$(URBS) (ANIMAL) EQUUS-sa$_8$ (*219)ha+ra/i-pa-zi/a-‹ha› OMNIS-MI-zi/a á-za$_5$-sa$_7$-na FINES+HI zi/a(-)CRUS+RA/I

§ 27 wa/i-ti-ia-na NEG$_2$+ra/i? x-i‹a?›+ra/i

§ 28 (DEUS)TONITRUS-hu-zi/a-sa$_4$-pa-wa/i-tú-ta$_x$ *273+RA/I.*200-na ARHA CAPERE-ta$_x$

§ 29 a-wa/i$_5$ NEG$_2$ REL$_x$-ha mu-wa/i-ta$_x$ i-zi/a-ia-tà

§ 30 á-mu-pa-wa/i (DEUS)TONITRUS-hu-sa|| (DEUS)SARMA-ma-sa (DEUS)*198-sa (DEUS)BOS.*206.PANIS-sa *273+RA/I.*200-na DARE-ta$_x$

§ 31 wa/i$_5$-mí-i á-x (DEUS)TONITRUS-hu-na (DEUS)SARMA-ma-na (DEUS)*198-na (DEUS)BOS.*206.PANIS-na á-ru?-na POST+ra/i-ta$_x$ CAPERE.ARGENTUM-‹x›-sà-wa/i$_5$

§ 32 á-ta$_4$/i$_4$-ha-wa/i-mu wa/i+ra/i-lí-na MAGNUS+ra/i-zi/a-na *273+RA/I.*200-na [...]-ti

§ 33 wa/i-mí á-ta$_4$/i$_4$ (DEUS)TONITRUS-hu-na (DEUS)SARMA-ma-na [... ||

§ 34 ...] CAPERE[...] REL$_x$‹-sà› ARHA ha+ra/i-ri+i

§ 35 wa/i-sa REL-i[...?] REX-ti-sa

§ 36 wa/i-ta$_x$ a-pa-sa-na COR-tara/i-i-na á-pa-sa$_7$-[ha?] TERRA-REL<+ra/i>-na (DEUS)TONITRUS-h[u-sa] (DEUS)SARMA-ma-sa$_6$ [(DEUS)*198-sa] (DEUS)BOS.[*206.]PANIS-sa ARHA ha+ra/i-tú-u

§ 37 REL$_x$-i[...?]-pa-wa/i-[sa] POST+ra/i-[sa] CAPUT-ti-[sa]

§ 38   wa/i-ta$_x$ á-pa-sa-na COR-tara/i-na a-pa-sa-ha DOMUS-
       na-zi/a (DEUS)TONITRUS-hu-sa (DEUS)SARMA-ma-sa
       (DEUS)*198-[sa] (DEUS)BOS.*206.PANIS-[sa-ha] AR[HA]
       ha+ra/i-t[ú-u]

       Scribal Signature:
§ 39   CAPERE+SCALPRUM-pa-wa/i+ra/i la-‹sa$_7$› wa/i$_4$-su-
       SARMA-ma-sa$_7$ MAGNUS.REX ... [...

§§ 1–6   [Great Ki]ng Wasusarmas, Great King, Hero, son of Tuwatis, Great King, Hero. In the presence of Muwaziti, Wasusarma ...ed.[57] And in the city Parzata(?),[58] eight kings, lower and more important ones, were hostile; three kings were friendly to me: Warpalawas,[59] Kiyakiyas,[60] and the charioteer(?)[61] Ruwatas. With the royal cavalry I myself brought and put (up) fortresses (as) my frontier posts.
§§ 7–15 The man from Parzata(?) ...ed (to) me at the frontier,[62] and he went (and) with all his cavalry and army raised his own frontier here, and he put (it) on the mountain. With my royal cavalry, I myself ...ed

---

57. Verb unclear.
58. The city name contains an uncertain sign, *432. Recently, Yakubovich has suggested a reading za$_x$ (2010a: 81–83). The city has been connected with the Hittite city of Purushanda, possibly to be identified with Acem Höyük or Karahöyük-Konya.
59. Warpalawas appears in Assyrian annals as Urballa, attested for the period ca. 738–709 B.C.E. He left two hieroglyphic inscriptions, BOR and İVRİZ 1.
60. Kiyakiyas can be identified as Kiakki of Šinuhtu, who was dethroned in 718 B.C.E. by Sargon II. He left one hieroglyphic inscription, AKSARAY.
61. This epithet is written with the logogram *91, which shows a foot above two wheels, and with a ladder-like object stretching from shin to toe. I understand this glyph as depicting a person by association and would like to suggest the following interpretation: The wheels underneath the foot symbolize the fact that the person referred to does not walk but moves on wheels. The ladder-like object might show the reigns a charioteer holds, a pars pro toto symbol of the person intended. I can see no obvious use for a ladder in this context.
62. I wonder whether, since the combination CAPERE+SCALPRUM, showing a hand with a chisel, means "to engrave," CURRUS+SCALPRUM could mean to drive so fiercely as to leave sander marks on the ground, i.e., "the man from Parzata drove very fiercely to me"?

(the ...),[63] and he ...ed twice(?),[64] ... I ...ed[65] down. He (the cavalry?) went into the land of Parzata(?) with strength, and burnt(?) buildings(?), and he reduced the region,[66] (including) women (and) children (to) servitude.

§§ 16-18 But afterwards, the Great ones (of the) cavalry watched the frontiers for me. My lord, the Storm God, Šarruma, the gods *198 and BOS.*266[67] ran before me,[68] and with a battle I was good (successful?).

§§ 19-24 And against him for two years, my royal cavalry, the First of the First(?), continually smote the city ... in the land. And against him for three years, they crossed(?) into the land (of) the city ..., and in the third year, the Great ones (of the) cavalry were of(?) ... with the First of the First. ...[69] And then he went down to the land of Parzata(?) with the following(?) cavalry, and he burnt the city [...].

§§ 25-30 But when he reduced region, women (and) children (to) servitude, the cavalry of the land of Parzata(?) and all the rebels attacked our frontier, but he (the enemy) did not take(?) it for himself. The Storm God took the victory away from him, and he made no conquest. But the Storm God, Šarruma, the gods *198 and BOS.*206 gave the victory to me.

§§ 31-33 In future, I myself shall ... the Storm God, Šarruma, the gods *198 and BOS.*206... in high measure,[70] and (Tarhunza) shall make great victory my own in high measure. And I for myself [shall ...] the Storm God, Šarruma, [the gods *198 and BOS.*206...] in high measure.

§§ 34-38 Who(soever) shall smash [this inscription?], if he (is) a king, may the Storm God, Šarruma, the gods *198 and BOS.*206 smash his person

---

63. Verb (and possible object) unknown; repeated two clauses further.
64. Verb unknown.
65. Repeats the verb of second to last clause, reaffirming the action taken by Wasusarmas with his cavalry.
66. Meaning its inhabitants?
67. The identity of the two gods written logographically as (DEUS)*198 and (DEUS)BOS.*206.PANIS remains uncertain. Suggestions include the grain god Halki for the former and Šauška for the latter but no obvious reading for these writings is forthcoming.
68. This is a recurring topos expressing divine preferment and assistance; compare in this volume also BABYLON 3, KARKAMIŠ A11b+c, TELL AHMAR 6 and ALEPPO 2.
69. An incomprehensible clause.
70. Cf. Rieken and Yakubovich 2010a: 213.

§ 39   [and] his land, but if he (is) a lesser man, may the Storm God, Šarruma, the gods *198 and BOS.*206 smash his person and his house!⁷¹
Las inscribed it, [...] of Wasusarmas, Great King [...

2.3. BUILDING INSCRIPTIONS

Without doubt, the majority of the surviving Hieroglyphic Luwian texts belong to the category of building inscriptions, often including historical narratives of varying length.

Building activities were part of a king's demonstration of wealth and strength, and the peace time counterpart to besieging and destroying cities. Newly conquered territories would have to be settled with loyal subjects and fortified, but kings also built and extended existing structures in their main cities, from religious foundations such as temples to domestic buildings such as the female quarters erected by Katuwas, king of Karkamiš.

As a literary genre, Luwian building inscriptions adhere to an archetypal pattern, although not all of the following elements may be present in shorter inscriptions. Firstly, the author relates his genealogy and states the building activity. Typically, this is followed by a historical narrative, recounting important events in the reign of this king, and frequently contrasting his achievements against those of his predecessors. This narrative may in turn lead up to a more detailed account of the building activity in question. A dedication to one or several deities forms the next part of such an inscription, and protective curses for both inscription and building conclude the text.

2.3.1. RESTAN, QAL'AT EL MUDIQ, TALL ŠṬĪB, HINES

The city of Hama (Luwian Imat, biblical Hamath), situated on the river Orontes, was the capital city of the small Neo-Hittite kingdom of Hama. A small group of hieroglyphic inscriptions attests two rulers, Urahilina (Irhuleni, ca. 853–845 B.C.E.) and his son Uratamis (ca. 840–820 B.C.E.). The Assyrian King Šalmaneser III records that Irhuleni and Ahab of Israel joined an Anti-Assyrian alliance, defeated at the battle of Qarqar (853 B.C.E.). This strengthens the identification of the Old Testament "Hittite kings" with the historical Neo-Hittite kings,

---

71. It is interesting that two curse formulae, each appropriate to the social standing of the offender, are used rather than a single, more general phrase (e.g., "his person and property"). Such juxtaposition of two participants is a frequent feature of Luwian inscriptions, cf., e.g., the contemplation of male and female malefactors in KARKAMIŠ A11b+c, §§ 26–29.

especially those of Hama. Around 800 B.C.E., the Luwian dynasty was replaced by Arameans. The following inscriptions of Urahilina are short texts,[72] containing only three clauses each, representing the most basic form of this genre. They comprise three elements, the author's genealogy, a mention of his building activity, and a dedication to a Semitic goddess, Ba'alat, who was worshipped as Pahalatis at Hama.

Two of these inscriptions are well preserved with relief script on the top part of rounded stelae: QAL'AT EL MUDIQ was excavated in 1937 to the North of Hama, while RESTAN, located to the south of Hama, near Homs, was already spotted in 1902. In 2002, a new and remarkably similar inscription was discovered at TALL ŠṬĪB,[73] 41 km north-northwest of Hama. The inscription from HINES differs in several ways. Its condition shows more wear, only preserving a few words in incised writing, yet enough to show that the visual arrangement of the inscription differed, for instance the line break occurred at a different place. How it came to be found in northern Iraq, where it was spotted in 1924 built into a village elder's house, is unknown.[74]

(RESTAN)

1 § 1 EGO-*mi u+ra/i-hi-li-na* PRAE-*tá-sa* ([INF]ANS)[*ni*]-*mu-wa/i-za-sa i-ma-tú-wa/i-ni*(REGIO) REX

2 § 2 *a-wa/i* || *za-na* "URBS+*MI*"-*ni-na* EGO AEDIFICARE+*MI-ha*

§ 3 *za-pa-wa/i* ("STELE")*wa/i-ni-za* (DEUS)*pa-ha-la-ti-ia* CRUS-*nu-ha-á*

(QAL'AT EL MUDIQ)

1 § 1 EGO-*mi u+ra/i-hi-li-na* PRAE-*tá-sa* (x) (INFANS)*ni-mu-wa/i-za-sa i-ma-tú-wa/i-ni*(REGIO) REX (x)

2 § 2 *a-wa/i* || *za-na* "URBS+*MI*"-*ni-i-na* EGO AEDIFICARE+*MI-ha*

§ 3 *za-pa-wa/i* ("STELE")*wa/i-ni-za* (DEUS)*pa-ha-la-ti-ia* CRUS-*nu-ha*

---

72. Cf. Yakubovich 2010b: 396 n. 9.

73. My transliteration is based on photographs kindly provided by Marie-Odile Rousset, © mission Marges arides.

74. Hawkins (2000: 409) hypothesizes that it might be a copy made in antiquity of an original inscription transferred to Assyria by either Shalmaneser III or Sargon II.

(TALL ŠṬĪB)

1   § 1   EGO-*mi u+ra/i-hi-li-na* PRAE-*tá-sa* [(INFANS)*ni-*]*mu-w*[*a/i*]-*za-sa i-ma-tú-wa/i-ni*(REGIO) REX ‖

2   § 2   *a-wa/i za-na* "URBS+*MI*"[-*ni*]-*na* EGO AEDIFICARE+*MI-ha*

     § 3   *za-pa-wa/i* ("STELE")*wa/i-ni-za* (DEUS)*pa-ha-la-ti-ia* CRUS-*nu-ha*

(HINES)

1–2   § 1   [...] (INFANS)*ni-mu-wa/i-za-sa*‖ *i-ma-tu-wa/i-ni*(REGIO) REX

     § 2   *a-wa/i za*[...

RESTAN

§ 1–3   I (am) Urahilina, son of Paritas, king of Hama. This city I built, and this stele I set up for Baʻalat.

QALʼAT EL MUDIQ

§§ 1–3   I (am) Urahilina, son of Paritas, king of Hama. This city I built, and this stele I set up for Baʻalat.

TALL ŠṬĪB

§§ 1–3   I (am) Urahilina, son of Paritas, king of Hama. This city I built, and this stele I set up for Baʻalat.

HINES

§§ 1–3   [I (am) Urahilina,] son [of Paritas,] king of Hama. This [city I built, and this stele I set up for Baʻalat.]

2.3.2. HAMA 1–3, 6–7

The following building inscriptions were set up by the other known Hamathite king, Uratamis (ca. 840–820 B.C.E.), Urahilina's son. In length and content they are similar to those of his father, the only differentiating feature within this group being the use of various geographical names. While not of great literary value, these inscriptions are historically important as they were the very first hieroglyphic texts noted by travelling scholars at the end of the nineteenth century, and they mark the beginning of a renewed interest in the hitherto almost forgotten world of the Hittites. News of inscriptions on building blocks from the Syrian city of Hama was first reported in 1812 C.E. In 1872, these inscriptions were recovered by the reverend William Wright, copied and casts taken, and the inscriptions removed to the Museum of İstanbul. Wright connected the writing with the Hittites, although initially it became known as "Hamathite writing." It is important to stress that at the time of their discovery, there was little cultural or linguistic context to these finds. The capital city Hattusa-Boğazköy of the Hittite Empire was yet to be discovered, and over the millennia, almost all knowledge of Hittite civilization had been obliterated save for a few biblical references (see 1.1).

(HAMA 1)

1 § 1 EGO-*mi* MAGNUS+*ra/i-tà-mi-sa u+ra/i-hi-li-na-sa* |INFANS. *NI-za-sa* [*i-ma-tú-wa/i-ni* REGIO REX]||

2 § 2 [*a-wa/i á-mu* AEDIFICARE+*MI-ha za-´*] ("CASTRUM") *ha+ra/i-ni-sà-za*

§ 3 *hu+ra/i-pa-tà-wa/i-ni-sa*(REGIO) FLUMEN.REGIO-*tà-i-sa* ||
3 REL-*za i-zi-i-tà*

§ 4 *a-tá-ha-wa/i* TONITRUS.*HALPA-pa-wa/i-ni-zi*(REGIO)

(HAMA 2)

1 § 1 EGO-*mi* MAGNUS+*ra/i-tà-mi-sa u+ra/i-hi-li-na-sa* |INFANS. *NI-za-sa i-ma-tú-wa/i-ni*(REGIO) REX ||

2 § 2 *a-wa/i á-mu* AEDIFICARE+*MI-ha za-´* ("CASTRUM") *ha+ra/i-ni-sà-za*

§ 3 *la-ka-wa/i-ni-sà-ha-wa/i*(REGIO) FLUMEN.REGIO-*tà-i-sà* ||
3 REL-*za i-zi-i-tà*

§ 4 *a-tá-ha-wa/i ni-ki-ma-sa*(REGIO)

(HAMA 3)

1 § 1 EGO-*mi* MAGNUS+*ra/i-tà-mi-sa u+ra/i-hi-li-na-sa* |INFANS. *NI-za-sa i-ma-tú-wa/i-ni*(REGIO) REX

2	§ 2	*a-wa/i* ‖ *á-mu* AEDIFICARE+*MI-ha za-'* ("CASTRUM") *ha+ra/i-ni-sà-za*
	§ 3	*mu-sa-ni-pa-wa/i-ni-sà*(REGIO) FLUMEN.REGIO-*sà* REL-*za i-zi-i-tà*

(HAMA 6)

1	§ 1	EGO-*mi* MAGNUS+*ra/i-tà-mi-sa u+ra/i-hi-li-na-sa* |INFANS.NI-*za-sa i-ma-tú-wa/i-ni*(REGIO) REX
2	§ 2	*a-wa/i* ‖ *á-mu* AEDIFICARE+*MI-ha za-'* ("CASTRUM") *ha+ra/i-ni-sà-za*
	§ 3	("*218")*ku-su-na-la-zi*(REGIO) REL-*za i-zi-ia-ta*

(HAMA 7)

1	§ 1	EGO-*mi* MAGNUS+*ra/i-tà-mi-sa u+ra/i-hi-li-na-sa* |INFANS.NI-*za-sa i-ma-tu-wa/i-ni*(REGIO) REX
2	§ 2	*a-wa/i á-mu* AEDIFICARE+*MI-ha* ‖ *za-'* ("CASTRUM") *ha+ra/i-ni-sà-za*
	§ 3	("MONS")*la-pa+ra/i-na-wa/i-ni-sa* FLUMEN.REGIO-*tà-i-sà* REL!?-*za i-zi-i-tà tú-ha-ia-ta-sa-ha*(REGIO)‖
3	§ 4	*a-tá-ha¹-wa/i ha¹-ma-ia+ra/i-sa*(REGIO)

HAMA 1

§§ 1–4 I (am) Uratamis, son of Urahilina, [king of Hama. I myself built this] fortress which he of the Hurpata river land made, and in addition the Halabeans.

HAMA 2

§§ 1–4 I (am) Uratamis, son of Urahilina, king of Hama. I myself built this fortress which he of the Laka river land made, and in addition the Land Nikima.

HAMA 3

§§ 1–3 I (am) Uratamis, son of Urahilina, king of Hama. I myself built this fortress which he of the Musanipa river land made.

HAMA 6

§§ 1–3   I (am) Uratamis, son of Urahilina, king of Hama. I myself built this fortress which the Kusunites made.

HAMA 7

§§ 1–4   I (am) Uratamis, son of Urahilina, king of Hama. I myself built this fortress which the river land of Mount Lab(a)r(a)na[75] made, and the land Tuhayata, and in addition the land Hamayara.

2.3.3. HAMA 4

This is a longer building inscription of Urahilina, which records the construction and endowment of a temple of the Semitic goddess Ba'alat.

A1	§ 1	EGO-*mi u+ra/i-hi-li-na* PRAE-*tá-sa* |INFANS.NI-‹*mu*›-*wa/i-za-sa i-ma-tu-wa/i-ni*(REGIO) REX
	§ 2	*a-wa/i* FRONS-*la/i/u* "X"(-)x-x-*sa*? NEG$_2$ x x x
	§ 3	*a-wa/i* VIR-*ti-zi* FEMINA-*ti-zi-ha zi-la-ta* PES$_2$-*tà-ta*‖ […
A2	§ 4	…] *á-mi-za á-mu-ha* *273.REX[-?]-*wa/i-ha á-mi* *336-*na-na*
	§ 5	*a-wa/i* DEUS-*ni* DEUS-*ni* REL-*ti-ha á-pi-si-na* "SOLIUM"-*sa-na i-zi-i-ha*
	§ 6	*za-pa-wa/i* "SOLIUM"-*sa-na* (DEUS)*pa-ha-la-ti-ia* AEDIFICARE+*MI-ha* ‖
A3	§ 7	*wa/i-ta* (DEUS)*pa-ha-la-ti-i-sà á-ma-za-ha-' á-ta$_5$/i$_5$-ma-za* PONERE-*ha*
	§ 8	*za-ti-pa-wa/i-ta* SOLIUM-*sa-' * REL-*i-sà* (DEUS)*pa-ha-la-ti-sà á-ma-za-ha á-ta$_5$/i$_5$-ma-za wa/i-na-ha* "CAPERE"-*ia*
	§ 9	*á-pi-pa-wa/i* (DEUS.TONITRUS)*tara/i-hu-za-sa* ‖ […
B1	§ 10	(DEUS)*pa-ha-la-ti-sà-pa-wa/i* DEUS.DOMUS+*MI-za á-mi-za*
B2		*tá-ti-za* AVUS-*ha*‖-*tà-za-ha-wa/i ara/i-za a+ra/i-tà a-tá* ("*218")*ta+ra/i-pa-ri+i-ta*

---

75. Labrana = Hittite Lablana, Mt. Lebanon? See Hawkins 2000, 414.

TEXTS 65

B3	§ 11	("BOS")*u-su-pa*‖*-ta-tà-ha-wa/i* ("FLAMMAE(?)")*la/i/u-za-li-na*
B4		NEG$_2$-′ ("FLAMMAE(?)")*la/i/u-sà-la/i/u-sà*‖*-ta* DEUS-*ni-i* SUPER+*ra/i-′* INFRA-*ta*
A4	§ 12	EGO-*pa-wa/i á-mi-za ara/i-za* ‖ NEG$_2$ *a-tá* ("*218")*ta+ra/i-pa-ri+i-ti ara/i-tà*
	§ 13	*wa/i-tú-ta* ("*163")*mu-ha-na* (VITIS)*sa$_5$+ra/i<-la>-ta-za-ha* PONERE-*ha ara/i-na ara/i-na*
	§ 14	("FLAMMAE(?)+*LA/I/U*")*la/i/u-za-li-ha-wa/i* "BOS"-*su-pa-ti-na* "BOS"-*na* ‖[...
		(erasure)
A5	§ 15	... *ara/i-la* ("PANIS")*tú+ra/i-pi-na* ("VITIS")*sa$_5$+ra/i-la-ta-za-ha-wa/i* ("*163")*mu-ha-ha-′*

§ 1	I (am) Urahilina, son of Paritas, king of Hama.
§§ 2–5	And at first ... not ..., and thereafter men and women walked ... .[76] ... I myself was king ...
§§ 5–7	And I made his own seat for every single god. But this seat I built for Ba'alat, and I put my name and Ba'alat's (on it).
§§ 8–12	But who(soever) shall take away[77] my name and Ba'alat's from this seat, but after(?), the Storm God Tarhunzas [...]. During the time of my father and grandfather, the temple of Ba'alat lacked income. They did not burn the burnt offering, a sacrificial ox,[78] up and down to the god. But (as regards) myself, in my times, it shall not lack income.
§§ 13–15	Time and time, I offered to it MUHA and offerings, and the [I ...ed] the burnt offering, a sacrificial ox. [...(erasure)...] bread and offerings and MUHA.

---

76. I tentatively understand this as a sentence contrasting life before and under the reign of this king (*hantili ... zilanda* ...); sense maybe "at first, men and women did not walk (peacefully), but then (in my times) men and women walked (peacefully). For a similar sentiment cf. KARATEPE §§ 33–35.

77. *wanaha* has recently been elucidated by Yakubovich as "away," cf. Hittite *awan arha* "away"; Yakubovich, forthcoming.

78. The term *usupatata* seems to refer to some kind of animal sacrifice, specifically cattle because of the determinative BOS; according to Yakubovich (pers. comm.), the stem contains the elements *u<*waw-* "cow" and *suppa-* "sacrificial meat," which would make good sense in this context.

2.3.4. KARKAMIŠ A11a

From the city of Karkamiš, once the seat of Hittite control over the Syrian territories, come several longer building inscriptions; they were inscribed on building blocks and other architectural elements. The following two long building inscriptions of the ruler Katuwas, son of Suhis, show the typical extended structure of the genre and contain information on the history of Karkamiš.

This inscription was found partially *in situ* at the "King's Gate" of Karkamiš, where it was used as a door jamb on the right side. It dates to the reign of Katuwas, ca. tenth–early-ninth century B.C.E.

1 § 1 EGO-*wa/i-mi* ¹*ka-tú-wa/i-sa* |(IUDEX)*tara/i-wa/i-ni-sa* |*kar-ka-mi-si-za-sa*(URBS) RE[GIO DOMINUS ... ¹*su-hi-si* REGIO DOMINUS]-‹*ia-i-sa*› [|(INF]ANS)*ni-mu-wa/i-za-sa* ¹*á-sa-tú-wa/i-ta₄/i₄-ma-za-si-i* |REGIO-*ní* DOMINUS-*ia-i-sa* |INFANS.NEPOS-*sa*

2 § 2a *wa/i-m*[*u-x*] DE[US... (b) ... "MA]NUS"-*tara/i-ti* |PUGN[US... || ...]

§ 3 [*wa/i-mu* ... *á-ma-za t*]*á-ti-ia-za* "LIGNUM"[...]-*za* [|]*pi-‹ia›-tá*

§ 4 *wa/i-mu-*a* DEUS-*ní-zi mi*¹⁺-*ia-ti-*a* <">IUSTITIA"-*wa/i-ní-ti* PUGNUS-*mi-la/i/u* |PUGNUS-*ri+i-ta*

§ 5 *mi-zi-pa-wa/i-mu-ta-*a* |20-*tá-ti-zi* ARHA CRUS+*RA/I*

§ 6 [*wa/i-m*]*a-tá-*[*a*]‹›REGIO-*ní-ia* |*314(-)*sá-pa-za* |REL-*a-ti* SUB-*na-na* ARHA (PES₂)*tara/i-za-nu-wa/i-tá*

§ 7 *wa/i-mu-*a mi-i-sa-*a* DOMINUS-*na-ni* || (DEUS)TONITRUS-*sa* (DEUS)*kar-hu-ha-sa* (DEUS)*ku+*AVIS-*pa-sa-ha mi-ia-ti-*a* |"IUSTITIA"-*na-ti* (LITUUS)*á-za-tá*

§ 8 *wa/i-mu-tá-*a á-ma* |*tá-ti-ia* AVUS-*ha-ti-ia* |REGIO-*ní-ia* (*33(1)*)mi-tà-sa₅+ra/i-i-na* REL-*a-ti a-tá i-zi-ia-tá*

§ 9 (DEUS)BONUS-*pa-wa/i-mu* (DEUS)"[VITIS]"(-)*t*[*i*-PR]AE-*i*[*a-ha* ...

§ 10 [*a*]-*wa/i mi-ia-za-*a* DEUS.AVIS-*ta-ní-ia-za* OV[IS...]-*wa/i* [ARGENTUM].DARE [x] ASINUS(ANIMAL) "HORDEUM"

4 || |CRUS+*RA/I*

TEXTS 67

§ 11 *mu-pa-wa/i-*a pi-na-*a* LINGERE-*sa-ti kar-ka-mi-si-za*(URBS) (DEUS)TONITRUS-*ti* DEUS.DOMUS-*tà* [*261.] PUGNUS-*ru-ha*

§ 12 *wa/i-tú-ta-*a* PANIS(-)*ara/i-si-na* PONERE-*wa/i-ha*

§ 13 |*za-ia-ha-wa/i* "PORTA"-*la/i/u-na á-ma* |AVUS-*ti-ia mu-*a* |PRAE-*na* CRUS.CRUS-*ta*

§ 14 *a-wa/i* PURUS-*MI-ia* DEUS.DOMUS-*sa*(?) *ku-ma-na* AEDIFICARE+*MI-ha*

§ 15 *wa/i-mu-tá-*a* |*za-zi* (SCALPRUM)*ku-ta-sa$_5$+ra/i-zi* |POST-*ní* || |PES-*wa/i-ta*

§ 16 *a-wa/i za-ia* "PORTA"-*na* |SCALPRUM-*sa$_5$+ra/i-ha*

§ 17 *wa/i-tà-*a* |FRONS-*la/i/u* ARGENTUM.DARE-*si-ia sa-tá-*a*

§ 18 *wa/i-tà-*a* "LIGNUM"-*wa/i-ia-ti* AEDIFICARE-*MI-ha*

§ 19 |*za-zi-pa-wa/i* (DOMUS)*ha+ra/i-sà-tá-ni-zi* ^{1}*á-na-ia* BONUS-*sa-mi-i* FEMINA-*ti-i* DOMUS+SCALA(-)*tá-wa/i-ni-zi i-zi-i-ha*

§ 20 |*za-ha-wa/i* (DEUS)*á-tara/i-su-ha-na za-ti-ia-za* |PORTA-*na-za* BONUS-*sa$_5$+ra/i-ti* (SOLIUM)*i-sà-nu-wa/i-ha*

§ 21 POST+*RA/I-wa/i-sà*<-*ti*?>-*pa-wa/i-tà* |REL-*a-ti* || PRAE-*na* CRUS.CRUS-*i*

§ 22 *wa/i-tà-*a* |SCRIBA+*RA/I* CAPERE-*i* REL-*i-sa*

§ 23 |*za-zi-pa-wa/i-tá* (SCALPRUM)*ku-ta-sa$_5$+ra/i-zi* LOCUS-*za-´* (SA$_4$)*sá-ní-ti*

§ 24 NEG$_2$-*pa-wa/i-tá* |*za-na* DEUS-*ní-na* LOCUS-*za-´* (SA$_4$)*sá-ni-ti*

§ 25 |NEG$_2$-*pa-wa/i-tá á-ma-za á-ta$_5$/i$_5$-ma-za* ARHA MALLEUS-*i*

§ 26 *wa/i-tú-ta-*a* (DEUS)TONITRUS-*sa* (DEUS)*kar-hu-ha-sa* (DEUS)*ku+*AVIS-*pa-sa-ha* LIS-*la/i/u-za-tú*

§ 27 *wa/i-tú-ta-*a* (PANIS)*tú+ra/i-pi-na* (LIBARE)*sa$_5$+ra/i-la*||-*ta-za-ha* NEG$_3$-*sa* ARHA |CAPERE-*ti-i*

§ 1 I (am) the ruler Katuwas, Coun[try-Lord] of Karkamiš, son [of the Country-Lord Suhis], grandson of the Country-Lord Astuwalamanzas.

§§ 2–4 The god[s ... raised] me by the hand, and they gave to me my paternal succession. And because of my justice the gods raised me in strength.

§§ 5–6   But my relatives(?) revolted against me, and therefore they caused the lands to break away[79] from under me.
§§ 7–10   My lord the Storm God, Karhuhas and Kubaba loved me because of my justice, and therefore made my father's and grandfather's lands MITASARI[80] for me. And for me [they brought forth] the Grain God and the Wine god, and in my days stood the cost for a sheep of [so many] homers barley.
§§ 11–13   But I myself then constructed(?) the temples for the Storm God of Karkamiš with that abundance, and I established for him seasonal bread (offerings). And these gates (of) my grandfathers passed down to me.
§§ 14–20   While I built the Holy (One's) temple, these orthostats came to me later, and I adorned these gates with orthostats.[81] They were very expensive: I built them with wood, and these upper floors I made into TAWANI[82] apartments for my beloved wife Anas. And I seated this god Atrisuhas[83] at these gates with goodness.
§§ 21–27   If in future they shall pass down to (one), who shall ..., and shall overturn these orthostats from (their) places, or shall overturn this god from (his) place, or shall erase my name, may the Storm God, Karhuhas, and Kubaba prosecute him! May they not accept from him bread and libation!

2.3.5. KARKAMIŠ A11b+c

This text is written on two portal orthostats, named A11b+c. The top of block c is damaged, causing a short break in our text. This six-line inscription relates the genealogy of its author, the ruler Katuwas (tenth or early-ninth century B.C.E.), and sums up historical events before detailing the building activity in question. We learn that times were uncomfortable but that Katuwas successfully defeated a revolt he faced. As expected, divine aid and preferment are named as major factors of the successful outcome. Katuwas records how he built upper floors to the city gates as women's quarters and established a procession and sacrifices for his main gods, Karhuhas and Kubabas. The text concludes with a long protec-

---

79. See Rieken 2004: 458–59.

80. This word remains unclear, but the context demands a positive meaning, as MITASARI is the result of the gods' favor.

81. Lit. "orthostated these gates."

82. DOMUS+SCALA(-)*tawani* is only elucidated by the context. The ladder (SCALA) of the logogram seems to reaffirm the upstairs factor of this habitation space.

83. The divine name Atrisuhas can be analysed as *atri=suhas*, "soul of Suhis," and seems to refer to the deified ancestor of Katuwas, the ruler Suhis.

tive curse formula and a summary of the main theme, the building of said upper floors.

A11b

1 §1 EGO-wa/i-mi ¹ka-tú-wa/i-sa "IUDEX"-ni-i-sa DEUS-ni-ti-i (LITUUS)á-za-mi-i-sa kar-ka-mi-si-za-sa(URBS) |REGIO-ni DOMINUS-sa ¹su-hi-si |REGIO-ni DOMINUS-ia-i-sa |INFANS.NI-za-sa ¹á-sa-tú-wa/i-ta₅/i₅-ma-za-si REGIO-ni DOMINUS-i-sa |INFANS.NEPOS-si-i-sa

   §2 a-wa/i za-a-sa URBS+MI-ni-i-sa mi-sá-*a |tá-tà-li-sa AVUS-ha-tà-li-sa || ¹*447-nu-wa/i-ia-si sa-tá-*a
2
   §3 wa/i-sa-*a VACUUS-ti-i-sa |ARHA ("LONGUS")ia+ra/i-ia-ta

   §4 wa/i-na-*a ¹MAGNUS+ra/i-TONITRUS-tá-sa-za |INFANS.NEPOS-sa-za CUM-ní |(LOCUS)pi-ta-ha-li-ia-ha

   §5 wa/i-ma-zá-*a mi-i-na-*a |sá-pa-ta₄/i₄-li-na |URBS+MI-ni i-pa-ni-si-ná(URBS) |á-ma-ha-wa/i |sá-pa-ta₄/i₄-li-ia TERRA.PONERE-ru-tà mu-zi-ki-ia(URBS) |[...]||

3 §6 wa/i-ma-na-*a |AEDIFICARE-MI-ha

   §7 a-wa/i |REL-a-ti-i |(ANNUS)u-si-i ka-wa/i-za-na(URBS) |(CURRUS)wa/i+ra/i-za-ni-ná |PES₂-za-ha

   §8 pa-tá-za-pa-wa/i-ta-*a (TERRA+LA+LA)wa/i-li-li-tà-za mi-i-zi-*a |tá-ti-i-zi AVUS-ha-ti-zi-ha |*348(-)la/i/u-tà-li-zi-ha |NEG₂-´ (PES₂)HWI-HWI-sà-tá-si

4 §9 mu-pa-wa/i-*a mi-i-sa-*a DOMINUS-na-ní-i-sa || CAELUM (DEUS)TONITRUS-sa (DEUS)kar-hu-ha-sá (DEUS)ku+AVIS-pa-pa-sa-ha mi-ia-ti-*a "IUSTITIA"-wa/i-na-ti (LITUUS)á-za-tá

   §10 wa/i-ma-tá-*a ("LIGNUM")hu-hú+ra/i-pa-li |(SOLIUM)á-sa-tá

   §11 wa/i-ma-tà-*a |PRAE-na (PES₂)HWI-ia-ta

   §12 a-wa/i pa-ia-*a |REGIO-ni-ia ("VACUUS")ta-na-tá-ha

   §13 wa/i-ta-*a (SCALPRUM.CAPERE₂)u-pa-ní-zi a-tá |("CAPERE₂")||u-pa-ha
5

§ 14   *a-wa/i pi-i-na-*a* |REGIO-*ni-ia-ti* (FULGUR)*pi-ha-mi-sa* SUPER+*ra/i-´* |PES-*wa/i-i-ha*

§ 15 |*za-zi-ha-wa/i-mi-i* (DOMUS.SUPER)*ha+ra/i-sà-tá-ni-zi pa-ti-i-*a* ("ANNUS")*u-si* |AEDIFICARE-*MI-ha*

§ 16   *wa/i-mi-ta-*a mi-i-na-*a* DOMINUS-*na-i-ni-i-na* (DEUS) *kar-hu-ha-si-na* (DEUS)*ku*+AVIS-*pa-si-ha* CRUS.CRUS(-)*ní-ia-sa-ha-na* |LITUUS+*na-ha*

§ 17   *wa/i-ma-tá-*a* |*za*||-*ti-i* |("PODIUM")*hu-ma-ti* |(SOLIUM) *i-sà-nú-wa/i-ha*

§ 18 a ("*350")*á-sa-ha+ra/i-mi-sà-pa-wa/i-ma-za* |*za-´* DEUS-*ní-za* |CUM-*ni* ANNUS-*sa-li-za-sa* |("PANIS")*tú+ra/i-pi-sa*

§ 18 b (DEUS)CERVUS$_2$+*ra/i-hu-ha-ia* 1 BOS(ANIMAL)-*sa* OVIS-*sa-ha*

§ 18 c (DEUS)*ku*+AVIS-*pa-pa* 1 BOS(ANIMAL)-*sa* 1 OVIS(ANIMAL)-*wa/i-sa-ha*

§ 18 d (DEUS)*sa$_5$+ra/i-ku* OVIS-*wa/i-sa* ("*478")*ku-tú-pi-li-sa-ha*

§ 18 e 1 OVIS(ANIMAL)-*wa/i-sa* |VIR-*ti-ia-tà-za* DEUS-*ní-za*||

A11c

§ 18 f [1 OVIS(ANIMAL)-*wa/i*]-*sa* [FEMINA-*ti*]-*ia*-[*ta*]-*za* [DEUS-*ni-za*]

...

§ 19   [...]-*sa z*[*a-ti*]-*ia-za* [DEUS-*n*]*i$^?$-za* MALUS-*ta$_4$/i$_4$-ti-i-´* || VERSUS-*ia-ni* |PES-*wa/i-ti*

§ 20 |NEG$_2$-*pa-wa/i-sa* |*za-ti-ia-za* (DOMUS.SUPER)*ha+ra/i-sà-tá-na-za* MALUS-*ta$_4$/i$_4$-ti-i-´* |VERSUS-*ia-ni* [PES]-*wa/i-ti*

§ 21   [|]NEG$_2$-[*pa*]-*wa/i-tà* CRUS.CRUS[(-)*ni$^?$*]-*ia-za-i* REL-*a-ti* PRAE-*na*

§ 22   [*wa/i*]-*tà-*a* [SCRIBA+*RA/I*] CAPERE-⟨*i*⟩ ⟨|⟩REL-*i-sa*

§ 23 |*za-a-zi-pa-wa/i-tá* [(SCALPRUM)]*ku-ta-sa$_5$+ra/i-zi-i* LOCUS-*ta$_4$/i$_4$-za* [...]||-*i-t*[*i*]

§ 24 |NEG$_2$-*pa-wa/i-tá* |*za-a-ti-ia-za* |("SCALPRUM") *ku-ta-sa$_5$+ra/i-za* |*á-ma-za* |*á-ta$_5$/i$_5$-ma-za* |ARHA |"MALLEUS"-*la/i/u-i*

	§ 25	*pa-ti-pa-wa/i-tá-*a* CAELUM (DEUS)TONITRUS-*sa* (DEUS)*kar-hu-ha-sá* (DEUS)*ku*+AVIS-*pa-pa-sá-ha* (MONS)*a+ra/i-pu-tá-wa/i-ni-sá-ha* (DEUS)TONITRUS-*sa* ("FLUMEN+MINUS")*sà-ku+ra/i-wa/i-ni-i-zi-ha* (FLUMEN.
4		REGIO)*ha*‖-*pa-tà-si* DEUS-*ní-zi* |LIS-*la/i/u-sa-tú*
	§ 26	*wa/i-tú-*a* |VIR-*ti-ia-ti-ia-za-ha* |("CULTER")*pa+ra/i-tú-ní-tú-u*
	§ 27	FEMINA-*ti-ia-ti-ia-za-ha-wa/i-tú-u* |("CULTER")*pa+ra/i-tú-ni-i-tú*
	§ 28	*wa/i-tú-´* |VIR-*ti-ia-ti-i-na* |(*462)*mu-wa/i-i-tà-na* NEG$_3$-*sa* |CAPERE-*ti-i*
5	§ 29	FEMINA-*ti-i*[*a*]-*ti-pa-wa/i-tú* (FEMINA.*462)‖4?-*tà* |*ni-i* |CAPERE-*ti-i*
	§ 30	|*za-pa-wa/i-tá* |URBS+MI-*ni-i-na mu-*a* |REL+*ra/i-i* ¹MAGNUS+*ra/i*-TONITRUS-*ta-sa-za* INFANS.NEPOS-*sa-za* |("*314")*ha-sá-ti-i* ARHA |CAPERE-*ha*
	§ 31	|NEG$_2$-*wa/i-na* |REL+*ra/i-i* (LOCUS)*pi-ta-ha-li-ia-ha*
	§ 32	*à-wa/i* |*za-a-zi* |DEUS-*ní-i-zi* |AUDIRE+MI-*ta+ra/i-ru*
6	§ 33	"LIGNUM"-*sa-pa*‖-*wa/i-mu-tá-´* |REL-*a-za za-a-ti-ia-za* |(DOMUS.SUPER)*ha+ra/i-sà-tá-na-za* POST-*ni* |PES-*wa/i-tà*
	§ 34	*a-wa/i* |*za-a-zi* "PORTA"-*la/i/u-ni-si-i-zi* (DOMUS.SUPER)*ha+ra/i-sà-tá-ní-zi* ¹*á-na-ia mi-i-*a* |BONUS-*sa-mi-i* FEMINA-*ti-i* |(BONUS)*wa/i-sa$_5$+ra/i-ti-i pa-ti-i-*a* |(ANNUS)*u-si-i* AEDIFICARE-MI-*h*[*a*]

§ 1   I (am) the ruler Katuwas, loved by the gods, Country-Lord of Karkamiš, son of the Country-Lord Suhis, grandson of the Country-Lord Astuwalamanzas.

§§ 2–8   This city of my father and grandfather belonged to Ninuwis,[84] but it stretched out empty. I ...ed it together with the grandsons of Ura-Tarhunzas, and from them [I ...ed] my SAPALALI city of Ipani and also my SAPALALI land(?)[85] of Muziki. I (re)built it for myself. In the

---

84. We do not know who Ninuwis is.
85. TERRA.PONERE-*ru-tà*, exact meaning unknown, stands parallel to the "city" and must therefore also mean some kind of territory.

	year in which I drove the city Kawa's chariotry (in) the city: to those fields my fathers, grandfathers and ancestors had not marched.
§§ 9-14	But because of my justice, my lord, celestial Tarhunzas, Karhuhas, and Kubabas loved me. For me they sat on the war chariot(?),[86] they ran before me. And I wasted the lands, and I brought the trophies inside, and I came up glorified from those lands.
§§ 15-18	These upper floors I built myself in that year, and I saw the procession of my lord Karhuhas and Kubabas for myself, and I seated them on this podium, and the sacrifice for them (shall be) this: with the gods annual bread, for Karhuhas, an ox and a sheep, for Kubabas, an ox and a sheep, for Sarkus, a sheep and a KUTUPILI,[87] one sheep for the male gods, [one she]ep for the fe[male gods, ...]
§§ 19-25	[... wh]o(?) comes towards these [gods] with badness, or comes towards these upper floors with badness, or if it shall pass down to (someone), who takes them/it ... and [overthr]ows these orthostats in their places or erases my name on these orthostats, against him let the celestial Tarhunzas, Karhuhas, and Kubabas, the Storm-God of the Arputaean mountain and the Sakuraean gods of the river land litigate!
§§ 26-29	Let them sever(?)[88] his masculinity, let them sever(?) her femininity, and they shall not take to him male seed, (or) take to her female seed!"
§§ 30-34	If I myself took away this city from Ura-Tarhunzas's grandsons by force, and did not ... it, let these gods be heard! Because wood came to[89] me afterwards for these upper floors, in that year I built these upper floors of the gates for my beloved wife Anas with goodness.

2.3.6. KARKAMIŠ A4d

This one-line inscription is an epigraph, a two-clause appendix to the inscription A11a, containing a god's curse on those who fail to make offerings to him. The inscription identifies the god as Atrisuhas,[90] and it was carved on the bottom of a statue, which showed the long-robed god sitting on his throne, with an axe in his

---

86. (LIGNUM)*huhurpali-* only occurs here. Melchert (1988: 229) interprets it as (part of) the war chariot, and the vivid imagery of the gods riding with Katuwas on his war chariot seems to fit well. But see also Rieken 1999: 452-54.

87. As the context moves from richer to lesser offerings, a KUTUPILI must be of lesser worth than a sheep, so either a younger or altogether smaller animal.

88. Exact meaning of (CULTER)*partuni-* unknown, but the determinative occurs in other inscriptions with the verb 'to cut."

89. See above, KARKAMIŠ A11a § 15.

90. Cf. KARKAMIŠ A11a § 20.

left and a mace in his right hand. The throne itself rested on a bird-headed figure holding a lion on either side. The monument was discovered during the Karkamiš excavation of 1911–1914 but is now lost.

§ 1   *za-[ti]-pa-wa/i* (DEUS)*á-tara/i-su-ha* DEUS-*ni-za* ‹CUM›-*ni* ANNUS-*sa-li-z[a]-n[a]* (PANIS) *tú+ra/i-p[i]-n[a]* BOS(ANIMAL) 2 OVIS(ANIMAL) REL-[*sa*] NEG$_{[2]}$ |[DARE]-*i*

§ 2   [*wa/i*]-*tú-tá-*a* (DEUS)*á-tara/i-su-ha-sa* |("CRUX")*wa/i-la/i/u* |PES-*wa/i-tú*

§§ 1–2   For this god Atrisuhas with the gods, (he) who does not [give] annual bread, an ox and two sheep: may Atrisuhas come fatally against him!

2.3.7. KARKAMIŠ A2+3

A long building inscription for the temple of the Storm God. The author Katuwas states his personal relationship with the Storm God and narrates how he built a temple as a thank offering for the Storm God's favors. The protective curse formula also informs us of the provisions Katuwas made for the temple.

A2

1   § 1   EGO ¹*ka-tu-wa/i-sa* |"IUDEX"-*sa kar-ka-mi-si-za-sa*(REGIO) REGIO DOMINUS-*ia-sa* ¹*su-hi-si-sa* |REGIO-*ni* DOMINUS-*ia-i-sa* |(INFANS)*ni-mu-wa/i-za-sa*

2   § 2   *wa/i-mu-*a* |*ku-ma-na* (DEUS)TONITRUS-*sa* || |*á-ma-za* |*tá-ti-ia*‹-*za*› |("LIGNUM")*sà-la-ha-za* |*pi-ia-ta*

§ 3   *a-wa/i* |*za-a-sa* |*kar-ka-mi-si-za-sa*(URBS) (DEUS)TONITRUS-*sa* NEG$_2$-*ha mi-i-*a* |*tá-ti-i* |"COR"-*tara/i-na* POST-*ni a-tá* |BONUS-*li-ia-ta*

§ 4   NEG$_2$-*ha-wa/i-sa mi-i-*a* AVUS-*ha* POST-*ni a-tá* |BONUS-*li-ia*||-*ta*

3

§ 5   *wa/i-sa-*a mu-*a ka-tu-wa/i-ia kar*‹-*ka*›-*mi-si-za*(URBS) REGIO DOMINUS-*ia* "COR"-*tara/i-na* POST-*ni a-tá* BONUS-*li-ia-ta*

§ 6   *wa/i-mu-ta* |*su-ha-na-ti-'*("FRONS")*ha-ta-ti a-tá* LITUUS+*na-tà*

4

§ 7   wa/i-ta-*a mi-ia-za-*a LITUUS+AVIS-ta-ni-ia-za |REGIO-ni-i a-tá (DEUS)BONUS-na (DEUS)VITIS(-)ti-PRAE-ia-ha|| ARHA (CAPERE$_2$)u-pa-ta

§ 8   a-wa/i mi-ia-za-*a |LITUUS+AVIS-ta-ni-ia-za |OVIS(ANIMAL)-i 10 ASINUS CRUS+RA/I

§ 9   mu-pa-wa/i-tu-*a |za-ia (DEUS)TONITRUS-sa DEUS.DOMUS-tà BONUS-sa$_5$<+ra/i>-ti-i za-la *261.PUGNUS-ru-ha

§ 10 á-ma-za-pa-wa/i-ta á-ta$_5$/i$_5$-ma-za REL-i-sa ARHA MALLEUS-i

5

§ 11 pa-ti-pa-wa/i-ta-*a |za-sa kar-ka-mi-si-za-sa(URBS) (DEUS)TONITRUS-sa || |("*464")ha-tà-ma |(PES$_2$.PES)tara/i-pi-i-tu

§ 12 wa/i-tu-ta-*a |LOCUS-ta$_5$/i$_5$-wa/i-za-ha |NEG$_3$-sa |CUM-i wa/i-sa-la-li-ti-i

§ 13 |POST+RA/I-wa/i-sà-ti-pa-wa/i |REL-sa |za-a-ia DEUS.DOMUS(-)ha-tà a-tá |*261(-)ta-pa-i

§ 14 a wa/i-sa-*a |ma-na REX-ti-sa||

6

§ 14 b |ma-pa-sa |REGIO DOMINUS-sa

§ 14 c |ma-pa-sa *355-li-sa

§ 15 wa/i-ta-*a pa-sa-*a |tá-ti-ia-za |DOMUS-ni-za |kar-ka-mi-si-za-sa(URBS) |DEUS.TONITRUS-sa |(CORNU)ki-pu-tà-ti-i a-tá |(PES$_2$.PES)tara/i-pi-tu-u||

A3

1

§ 16 |za-ti-pa-wa/i |kar-ka-mi-si-za(URBS) (DEUS)TONITRUS-ti-i ^{1}ka-tu-wa/i-sa |REGIO-ni-ia-si |DOMINUS-ia-sa REL-i-zi |("*273")wa/i+ra/i-pa-si |DOMINUS-ia-zi-i pi-ia-tá

§ 17 a ma-wa/i-sa |(CAELUM.*286.x)sá-pa-tara/i-i-sa

2

b |ma-pa-wa/i-sa |(*265)||mi-zi-na-la-sa

c |ma-pa-wa/i-sa |(SCUTELLA)tu-ni-ka-la-sa

d ma-pa-wa/i-tà |(DIES.OVIS)ku-ki-sà-ti-zi

e |MAGNUS+ra/i-hi-sa$_5$+ra/i-ma-sa-wa/i-tá$^{?1}$(URBS) |URBS(-)hu-tá-ni-i |REL-i-zi |SOLIUM+MI-ti

TEXTS

|§ 18 |POST+*RA/I-wa/i-sà-ti-pa-wa/i-ma-za-*a* |REL-*i-sa* |POST-*ni* |*a-tá* CRUS-*i*||

3 § 19 a |*ma-wa/i-sa* REX-*ti-sa*

    b   *ma-pa-wa/i-sa* |REGIO-*ni-ia-si* DOMINUS-*ia-sa*

§ 20   *wa/i-tà-tá-*a* |*za-a-ti-i* (DEUS)TONITRUS-*ti-i ARHA* |CAPERE-*i*

§ 21 |*pa-pa-wa/i-*a* |*za-a-sa* (DEUS)TONITRUS-*sa* (LOQUI)*tá-tara/i-ia-tu*

§ 22   *wa/i-sa-*a* |*ku-ma-na sa-ti-*a* |*pa-la-sa-ti-i*

4 § 23   *a-wa/i* (DEUS)TONITRUS-*sa*|| (DEUS)*ku+*AVIS-*pa-sa* |("FRONS")*ha-tá* |NEG$_3$-*sa* |LITUUS+*na-ti-i*

§ 24   *wa/i-sa-*a* |DEUS-*na-za* |CAPUT-*tá-za-ha* |*366-*na-na* |(DEUS)TONITRUS-*tá-ti-i* |(LOQUI)*ta-tara/i-ia-mi-sa i-zi-ia-ru*

§ 1   I (am) the ruler Katuwas, Country-Lord of Karkamiš, son of the Country-Lord Suhis.

§§ 2–5   When the Storm God gave me my paternal succession, this Storm God of Karkamiš had exalted the person neither for my father, nor for my grandfather had he exalted (it), but for me, Katuwas the Country-Lord of Karkamiš, he exalted the person.

§§ 6–9   And he regarded me with a smiling(?) face and in my days brought forth the Grain God and the Wine God in the country. In my days ten homers (of barley) stood for a sheep. And I myself then constructed(?) these temples for the Storm God with goodness.

§§ 10–15   But who(ever) erases my name, for him may this Storm God of Karkamiš trample on the ruins! May he not even WASALALI[91] his place(?)! In future, who(ever) shall block up these temples, whether he (be) a king, or he (be) a Country-Lord, or he (be) a priest, may the Storm God of Karkamiš trample the house of his father in(to the ground) with (his) hooves!

---

91. Hapax legomenon.

§§ 16-21[92] The Country-Lord Katuwas gave those who were master craftsmen to this Storm God of Karkamiš.[93] Whether one (be) a libation priest(?),[94] or whether one (be) a MIZINALA,[95] or whether one (be) a baker,[96] or whether they (be) KUKUSATIs,[97] who live in the village of Urhisarmas: whoever goes after them in future, whether he (be) a king, or whether he (be) a country lord, and takes them away from this Storm God of Karkamiš, may this Storm God of Karkamiš curse him!

§§ 22-24 When he shall be dead,[98] let him not behold the faces of the Storm God and Kubaba, and let him be made accursed by the Storm God before gods and men!

2.3.8. CEKKE

We have several interesting inscriptions dating to the reign of Kamanis, ruler of Karkamiš, among them two sales documents (KARKAMIŠ A4a; TÜNP 1) and this stela, which contains two separate inscriptions: a short dedication to the Storm God, which includes provisions for offerings. Secondly, there is the foundation deed of the city Kamana, presumably named after Kamanis. It may be debatable whether we should classify this as a building inscription proper, as it is concerned with the foundation of a city rather than building specific structures; I felt it was close enough to this genre to be considered here, especially as it offers

---

92. Katuwazas stipulates that the craftsmen whom he assigns to serve the Storm God's temple must never work for another master.

93. In the following, Katuwazas stipulates that the craftsmen whom he assigned to serve the Storm God's temple must never work for another master.

94. I would argue that both logogram and the phonetic word shape argue for an interpretation "libation priest." *sapantari-* might be connected to Hitt. *ispand-/išpant-* "to libate." The logogram (CAELUM.*286.X) seems to mark the divine sphere with the sign for heaven and shows a vessel shape, hieroglyph *286. Thus also Giusfredi 2010: 123.

95. Hapax legomenon. Giusfredi (2010: 153) suggests a connection with the PIE root *meik* "mix" but leaves open what kind of "mixer" the MIZINALA might be.

96. (SCUTELLA)*tunikala-*, "maker of *tunik*-bread."

97. Someone connected with sheep, as the determinative (DIES.OVIS) and the appearance of the term in an economic document concerned with sheep proves (KULULU lead strip); further, such a person was important enough to carry a seal (DÜLÜK and GAZİANTEP seals). His daily/daytime(?) (determinative DIES) occupation with sheep might equally concern their welfare as a shepherd or (ritual?) butchery. Giusfredi (2010: 150-51) prefers the latter on the basis of a tentative connection with Hittite *kukus-* 'to destroy."

98. Lit. "off the path," since life was viewed as a path given to a person by the gods, see Melchert 2010: 7-8.

a slightly different subject matter. We learn how the city was bought and how much it cost, the details of its foundation. The text names various fathers and sons connected with the city and concludes with a protective curse.

Inscription 1, obverse (bottom)

1–2	§ 1	EGO-*mi* DOMINUS.SOL‖-*wa/i+ra/i-sá sa-sa-tù+ra/i-sá wá/í-*
3		*sa*‖-*mi-sa* SERVUS-*ta$_5$/i$_5$*
4	§ 2	*a-wa/i* ‖ *za* LIGNUM[x]-‹*pa›-ma-za* ‹DOMINUS›. SOL-*wa/i+ra/i-sá sa-sa-*‹*tù+ra/i›-ia* ‖‹DOMINUS›-*ni á-pa-sa-na* PONERE-*tá*
	§ 3	|*za-ha-wa/i* STELE-*zi$^{?!}$ á-pa-sa pu-pa-li-tá*

(top)

1	§ 4	*za-ti-pa* CAELUM (DEUS)TONITRUS VITELLUS
2		(ANIMAL) *ARHA* ("[FLAMM]AE(?)")*k*[*i*‖-*n*]*u-ti*
	§ 5	POST+*ra/i-tá-pa-wa/i* BOS(ANIMAL) OVIS(ANIMAL)‖
3		LIBARE(-)*sa$_5$+ra/i-la-ti*

Inscription 2, reverse

1	§ 6 a	*ka-ma-ní-sa* IUDEX-*sa kar-ka-mi-sà*(URBS) *MA$_x$-zá*(URBS) REGIO.DOMINUS *sa-sá-tù+ra/i-sa* ¹*ka-ma-ní-sa* FRONS-*la/i/u-sa* SERVUS-*ta$_4$/i$_4$*
2	b	*ka-ma-na-na*(URBS) URBS+MI-*ní-na ka-na*‖-*pu-wa/i-na-za*(URBS) CUM-*ni* ("CONTRACTUS")*i-sa-ta á-pa-sa-ti* *314(-)*sa-tá-na-ti*
	§ 7	*wa/i-ma-za* 600 ASINUS(ANIMAL)-*i-za* DARE-*tá*
	§ 8	|*za-*CRUS+*RA/I-pa-wa/i* SUB$^{?!}$-*ní* 1 "ARGENTUM"-*ri+i* 3 (SCALPRUM)*ma-na-zi* ARGENTUM-*za* ¹*wa/i+ra/i-pa-tá*‖-*sa-za* INFANS.*NÍ-wa/i-za* DARE-*mi-na*
3		
	§ 9	|*há-ia-la* ¹*la-pa+ra/i-na-ia* ¹*za-za-ia-ha* 4 (SCALPRUM) *ma-na-zi* ARGENTUM-*za* (*349)*nú-hu-za-ti*(URBS) DARE-*mi-na*
	§ 10	|*há-ia-la* URBS+MI-*ni ta-ní-mi* ¹*á-ha-li-ia* FLUMEN.DOMINUS PRAE-*na* ‖ (PANIS.PITHOS)*á-zá-li-za i-zi-ia-mi-na*
4		

§ 11 wa/i BOS(ANIMAL) 15 OVIS ka-na-pu-ia(URBS) 2 SCAL-PRUM-na-zi ARGENTUM-za (PANIS.PITHOS)á-zá-li-sá DARE-mi-na

§ 12 DOMINUS-ti-wa/i+ra/i-ia-pa-wa/i á-ha-li-sa-na PRAE-ti *179.*347.5-sà-pa-sá 1 SCALPRUM-sa (*33(2)) mi+ra/i-sa₅+ra/i-zi DARE-mi-na

§ 13 URBS+MI-ní-pa-wa/i 20 tá-mi 10 INFANS-ní ki-tara/i-sa‖ (PUGNUS+PUGNUS)hi-sà-hi-mi-na

§ 14 (LIGNUM)ha-za-ni-sa-pa-wa/i za-sa(-)ha-pu-zi-sa INFANS.NI-wa/i-za-sa á-sa-ta BRACCHIUM-la/i/u-‹x›-ní-sa MAGNUS+ra/i-ia-zi-ha

§ 15 a-wa/i FINES-ha+ra/i-ia(-)ta-sa ha-zi-mi-na

§ 16 |wa/i-ta tá-ra+a-za |INFANS.NI-wa/i-za-ha ki-tara/i-sa (PUGNUS+PUGNUS)hi-sà-hi-mi-na

§ 17 a zi-la-pa+ra/i-ha+ra/i(URBS) TONITRUS-hu-ti-wa/i+ra/i-sá ¹hara/i-na-(m)u²-sa-ha |INFANS.NI-wa/i-za-sa á-pa-sá

§ 17 b ¹ha+ra/i‖-li-sa TONITRUS-hu-tá-wa/i+ra/i-sa-ha |INFANS.NÍ-za-sa á-pa-sá

§ 17 c ¹ha+ra/i-ní-sa ha-wa/i+ra/i-zá-sa(URBS) ¹sà-tá-|FRATER.LA-sa-ha |INFANS.NI-za-sa á-pa-sá

§ 17 d na-ni-sa |FRATER.LA-wa/i+ra/i-sa-ha |INFANS.NÍ-za-sa á-pa-sá

§ 17 e ‹la/i/u-tà›-pa-ti(URBS) ¹ka-mara/i-sa ¹REL-za-ia+ra/i-sa-ha |INFANS.NI-zá-sá á-pa-sá

§ 17 f PUGNUS-ri+i-mi-sá za-ha-mu-sa-ha‖ |INFANS.NI-za-sa á-pa-sa

§ 17 g á-pa-ku-ru-tà-ri+i(URBS) PUGNUS-mi-la/i/u-li-sa zú-zi-sa-ha |INFANS.NI-za-sa á-pa-sá

§ 17 h za+ra/i-ha-nu-ri+i(URBS) la-sá pi-ia-TONITRUS-hu-zá-sá-ha | INFANS.NI -za-sa á-pa-sá

§ 17 i SOL-wa/i+ra/i-mi-sá ¹sà-tá-(m)u²-sá-ha | INFANS.NI-za-sa á-pa-sá ‖

§ 17 j sa₅+ra/i-mu-tara/i(URBS) pa-pi-sá AVUS-ha-wa/i+ra/i-sa-ha |INFANS.NÍ-za-sa á-pa-sa

§ 17 k   TONITRUS.*HALPA-pa-mu-sa á-sa-ti*-TONITRUS-*za-sá-ha*
         <INFANS.*NI-za-sa*> *á-pa-sa*

§ 17 l   *i-sa-tara/i*(URBS) MAGNUS+*ra/i*-TONITRUS-*sa* TONI-
         TRUS-*hu-wa/i-su-wa/i-sa* | INFANS.*NÍ-za-sa á-pa-sá*||

§ 17 m   OMNIS-*mi*-|FRATER.*LA-sa* PUGNUS-*ri+i-mi-sá-ha* |
         INFANS.*NI-za-sa* <*á-pa-sa*>

§ 17 n   *hu-hu+ra/i-tà-ti*(URBS) ¹*á-mu-sa wa/i-li-na-ia-sa-ha* |
         INFANS.*NI-za-sa á-pa-sá*

§ 17 o   *sa-tara/i-pa-ti*(URBS) *za₅-na-(m)u²-sa* TONITRUS.*HALPA-
         pa*-SOL-*wa/i+ra/i-sá-ha* | INFANS.*NÍ-za-sa á-pa-sá*

§ 18 |*wa/i-tá su+ra/i-i-zi* || ("CAPUT")*ha-ra/i-ma-hi*
         MANUS.*311(-)*la/i/u²-mi-na*

§ 19   *a-wa/i* FINES-*hi-zi* PONERE-*mi-na*

§ 20 |*za-ti-pa-wa/i* URBS+*MI-ni* REL-*sa* MALUS-*hi-tà-ri+i*
         VERSUS (PES₂)*i+ra/i*

§ 21   *ni-pa-wa/i* FINES-*hi-zi* ARHA MANUS.*218(-)*la/i/u²-ha-i*

§ 22 |*ní-pa-wa/i-sa za-ti* STELE-*ri+i* (SCALPRUM)*tara/i-pi* ||
         CRUS-*ia*

§ 23   *wa/i-ta za-ia mara/i-ta* ARHA MALLEUS-*i*

§ 24   *á-pa-ti-pa-wa/i* CAELUM (DEUS)TONITRUS (DEUS)
         ka+ra/i-hu-ha-sá (DEUS)*ku*-AVIS-*ha* (DEUS)BONUS
         (DEUS)*i-sa-ha* (DEUS)LUNA+*MI-sa* (DEUS)SOL (CRUX)
         wa/i-la "PES"-*wa/i-tú*

§ 25   *a-wa/i* |"CAELUM"-*sa* CORNU+*RA/I-na* |*ni* LITUUS+*na-ti*

§ 26   TERRA-*pa-wa/i* CORNU+*RA/I-na* |*ní* || (PES₂.PES)[*tara/i-pi-
         ti*]

§ 27   (DEUS)*ku-pa*-AVIS-*pa-si-pa-wa/i* *476-wá/í-sa-ha-na*
         CORNU+*RA/I-na* |*ní* LITUUS+*na-ti*

§ 28   *wa/i-tú-tá za-zi* DEUS-*ní-zi* |"TERRA"-*sa* *185(-)*hu-sa-za*
         SCALPRUM-*na* x *á*-[…] ARHA *i-zi-ia-tú*

Inscription 1

§§ 1–5   I (am) DOMINUS-tiwaris,[99] beloved servant of Sasturas. DOMINUS-tiwaris set up this object(?)[100] for his lord Sasturas, and he (Sasturas) inscribed this stele. They shall burn a calf for this Storm God of Heaven, and in future, they shall offer an ox and a sheep.

Inscription 2

§§ 6–7   The ruler Kamanis, Country-Lord of the cities Karkamiš (and) Malizi(?), and Sasturas, first servant of Kamanis, bought the city Kamana from the men of Kanapu with their ..., and they gave 600 mules to them.[101]

§§ 8–12[102] ... from 1 ARGENTUM[103] 3 minas (of) silver are to be given to the sons of Warpatas, ... 4 minas (of) silver are to be given from the city Nuhuza to Labarnas and Zazas, ... a banquet is to be made in every city before the River-Lord Ahalis. An ox, 15 sheep are to be given to the city Kanapu, 2 minas (of) silver of the banquet. And before LORD-tiwaris, son of Ahalis, ... is to be given.

§§ 13–16 The city is to be bound (as) a donation for 20 TAMIS and 10 children,[104] and the mayor there was[105] Zas, son of Hapuzis, the BRACCHIUM,[106] and the great ones. Frontier stelae are to be engraved, and bound (as) a donation for fathers and sons:

---

99. Written logographically as DOMINUS.SOL.
100. Word not entirely clear but must refer to the inscription.
101. Hawkins (2000: 145) understands the following passage as quoted speech delivered with the payment of 600 mules.
102. The text switches person and tense; the present might equally have been used to indicate future stipulations or state present deeds.
103. ARGENTUM: a unit of weight measurement for silver, see Giusfredi (2010: 180–81).
104. If we understand this sentence to refer to the father-son pairs mentioned and named in the following clauses, Hawkins's suggestion to amend the unknown *tá-mi* to *ta-ti!*, "father" is preferable (2000: 149). If the numbers preceding the relationship terms (20 fathers 10 children) can be understood as 20+10, i.e., 30 fathers + children as per Hawkins, this would make for strange arithmetic but it is the only sensible interpretation in view of the following 15 father-son pairs.
105. Why the sudden use of the past tense? Does this mean Zas was but is no longer the mayor?
106. Alternatively, the mayor might be BRACCHIUM, son of Zashapuzis; see Hawkins 2010: 150.

§ 17 From the city Zilaparaha: Tarhuntiwaris and his son Haranamus, Haralis and his son Tarhuntawaris, Haranis of Hawara and his son Santadalas, Nanis and his son Adalawaris.
From the city Lutapa(?): Kamaras and his son Kwazayaras, Arimis(?) and his son Zahamus.
From the city Apakuruta: ...lumilis(?) and his son Zuzis.
From the city Zarahanu: Las and his son Piyatarhunzas, Tiwarimis and his son Santamus(?).
From the city Sarmuta: Papis and his son Huhawaris, Halpamus and his son Astitarhunzas.
From the city Isata: Uratarhunzas and his son Tarhuwasuwas, Tanimadalas(?) and his son Arimis(?).
From the city Huhurata: Amus and his son Walinayas.
From the city Satarpa: Zanamus(?) and his son Halpatiwaras.

§§ 18-19 ... the SURIs are to be ...ed at the head(?), and frontiers are to be established.

§§ 20-28 Who(ever) shall approach this city with malice, or shall infringe the borders, or shall stand up for crushing this stele,[107] and erase these words, may the heavenly Storm God, Karhuhas, and Kubaba, the Good God and Ea, the Moon (and) the Sun come fatally against him! Let him not behold the abundance of the Sky, and let him not tread on the abundance of the earth! And let him not behold the holy(?)[108] abundance of Kubaba! May these gods change the land's life (to) stone for him.

2.3.9. KARKAMIŠ A6

This building inscription was erected by Yariris, a most interesting historical figure who acted as regent and guardian to the children of the deceased king Astiruwas. This texts comments on his relationship with his ward Kamanis, son of Astiruwas, who would eventually succeed Yariris. The latter's loyalty to the ruling house might be explained by the fact that he was a eunuch and could therefore not start his own dynasty.

---

107. Cf. Yakubovich (2002: 208), who connects the determinative SCALPRUM "stone" with a more general meaning of the verb *tarp-* "to plough." Taking into consideration the use of SCALPRUM to determine or write other verbs, such as (CAPERE+SCALPRUM)*kwaza-* "to engrave" and CURRUS.SCALPRUM (see above, TOPADA § 7) "drive fiercely(?)," this determinative seems to symbolize both the material and its destructive force, further supporting Yakubovich's translation.

108. Cf. Hawkins 2000: 340; Giusfredi 2010: 258.

1	§ 1	|EGO-wa/i-mi-i ¹i-a+ra/i-ri+i-i-sa |IUDEX-ni-sa DEUS.AVIS-ta-ni-sà-mi-i-sa |LITUUS+ta-sa-pa-CERVUS-wa/i-ti-i-sa CAPUT-ti-i-sá ("OCCIDENS")i-pa-ma-ti-i (DEUS.ORIENS) ki-sá-ta-ma-ti-i |PRAE-ia |AUDIRE+MI-ma-ti-mi-i-sa DEUS-na-ti-i (LITUUS)á-za-mi-sa ‹CAPUT?›-ti-i-sa
2	§ 2	a-wa/i [x]-‹x›-zi [á]-ma-[za] [á-ta$_5$/i$_5$]-ma-[z]a || á-mi-ia-ti-i |IUSTITIA-na-ti (DEUS)TONITRUS-hu-za-sa (DEUS)SOL-wa/i-za-sa-ha ("CAELUM")ti-pa-si |"PES$_2$"(-)hi-nu-wa/i-ta-´
	§ 3	á-ma-za-ha-wa/i-ta á-ta$_5$/i$_5$-ma-za DEUS-ni-zi FINES+hi-ti-i-na |"PES$_2$"(-)hi-i-nu-wa/i-tá
	§ 4	wa/i-ma-ta$_5$/i$_5$ |zi-i-na ("MÍ.REGIO")mi-za+ra/i(URBS) |AUDIRE-MI-ti-i-ta
	§ 5	zi-pa-wa/i+ra/i |*475-la(URBS)-´ |AUDIRE+MI-ti-i-ta ||
3	§ 6	zi-i-pa-wa/i-´ mu-sá-za(URBS) mu-sà-ka-za(URBS) su+ra/i-za-ha(URBS) AUDIRE+MI-ti-i-ta
	§ 7	wa/i-ta ta-ni-mi REX-ti SERVUS-ta$_4$/i$_4$-ti-i-zi |a-ta (BONUS) wa/i-sa$_5$+ra/i-nu-ha
	§ 8	za-a-pa-wa/i ("MENSA.SOLIUM")á-sa-na-´ |ku-ma-na ¹ka-ma-ni-i-ia |á-mi-i-´ DOMINUS-na-ni |INFANS-ní |REL-i-ia AEDIFICARE+MI-ha
4	§ 9	|wa/i-sá |za-ti LOCUS-ta$_4$/i$_4$-ti-i |("PES$_2$")HWI-HWI-ta
	§ 10	|wa/i-ná |SUPER-la-ia |(["]SOLIUM")i-sà-nu-wa/i-ha
	§ 11	|a-wa/i ta-ní-mi |SUPER+ra/i-´ |("PES$_2$+PES")tara/i-pa-ta$_5$/i$_5$
	§ 12	|INFANS-ní-i-sa-wa/i-sá |REL-za |á-sa-ta-´
	§ 13	CUM-ni-pa-wa/i-tú-ta-´ |á-pa-sá |FRATER.LA-zi-i |i-zi-i-ha
5	§ 14	|a-wa/i |REL|-i-zi |("*314")ka-tú-na-sa
	§ 15	i-zi-i-sa-ta+ra/i-wa/i-ma-za |zi-la |("*314")ka-tú-ni-zi |(MANUS)i-sà-tara/i-i ("PONERE")tú-wa/i-há
	§ 16	REL-zi-pa-wa/i-ma-za-´ |("LIGNUM")tara/i-pu-na-sá
	§ 17	|i-zi-i-sa-ta+ra/i-wa/i-ma-za |zi-la |("LIGNUM")tara/i-pu-na-zi-i |(MANUS)i-sà-tara/i-i "PONERE"-wa/i-ha-´ ||
6	§ 18	¹ka-ma-ni-sa-pa-wa/i |REL-i-´ |INFANS-ní-sa |á-sa-tá

§ 19 |wa/i-ná ara/i-la-' ("3")tara/i-su-u "4"-su-u |("MANUS") pa+ra/i-si ("CRUS")ta-nu-wa/i-wa/i-i

§ 20 |wa/i-ta (DEUS)TONITRUS-hu-ti-i (DEUS)SOL-ti-i (DEUS)ku+AVIS-pa-pa-ia-ha ta-ni-mi-i-ha-a-wa/i || DEUS-ni-i |FRONS-ti-i |SUPER+ra/i-a-ta$_5$/i$_5$ PUGNUS-ri+i-wa/i

§ 21 |a-wa/i (LOQUI)ha+ra/i-nu-wa/i (DEUS)ku+AVIS-pa-pa-'

§ 22   u-za$_5$-sa-wa/i-ma-ta-' (MANUS)i-sà-tara/i-i |MAGNUS+ra/i-nu-wa/i-ta-ni-i

§ 23 |wa/i-sá |za-ti LOCUS-ta$_4$/i$_4$-ti |REL-i-' PES$_2$(-)HWI-ia-ta

§ 24 |wa/i-tú-u |za-na ("MENSA.SOLIUM")á-sa-na || AEDIFICARE+MI-ha

§ 25   za-sa-pa-wa/i (MENSA.SOLIUM)á-sa-sa CRUS+CRUS(-)ni-za-ia |REL-a-ti REL-ti-i-ha REX-ti |PRAE-na

§ 26   wa-ara/i |SCRIBA+RA/I CAPERE-i |REL-sa

§ 27 |zi-i-pa-wa/i |"SCALPRUM"-su-wa/i-ti-i |"SCALPRUM"-su-na-' |NEG$_3$-i CUM-ní ARHA |CAPERE-ia

§ 28 |ta-sà-pa-wa/i-' ta-si |NEG$_3$ CUM-ni ARHA |CAPERE-ia ||

§ 29 |ní-pa-wa/i-ta |á-ma-za |á-ta$_5$/i$_5$-ma-za-' |REL-i-sá |ARHA "MALLEUS"-la<-i>

§ 30 |ni-pa-wa/i |INFANS.NI-na-ti-i |zi-i-na |ni-pa-wa/i ("*474") wa/i-si-na-sa-ti zi-na REL-sa CUM-ni ARHA |CAPERE-ia

§ 31   á-pa-pa-wa/i-' (DEUS)ni-ka+ra/i-wa/i-sá CANIS-ni-i-zi á-pa-si-na |CAPUT-hi-na |ARHA EDERE-tú

§§ 1–7   I (am) the ruler Yariris, the ... ... prince, the prince(?) known in the west and the east, beloved by the gods. And ... because of my justice, the Storm God and the Sun caused my name to pass to heaven, and the gods caused my name to pass abroad, and men heard my (name) on the one hand in Mizra (Egypt), and on the other hand they heard it in *475-la,[109] and on the other hand they heard (it) among the Musa

---

109. Unless we assume that Babylon had two different part-logographic writings, seal evidence for the city name written with the sign*292, HAL-la, speaks against Bossert's suggestion to read here Babylon, as quoted by Hawkins (2000: 126). Starke (1997: 386) argues that *475-la(URBS) represents Urartu; if correct, this would prevent an identification of Sura with Urartu; see below.

(Lydians), the Muska (Phrygians) and the Sura,[110] and for every king I caused the subjects(?) to benefit(?).

§§ 8-17 And when I built this seat for my lord's child Kamanis, he used to run to this precinct. I made him sit high, and he trampled over all, while he was a child. And with him I made his brothers.[111] And (those) who are of KATUNI, I then put KATUNI in their hand(s) with honor, and (those) who are of TARPUNA, I then put TARPUNAs in their hand(s) with honor.[112]

§§ 18-22 And although Kamanis was a child, in time I shall cause him to stand three times, four times on (his) path. I shall raise(?) them[113] up before the Storm God, the Sun and Kubaba and every god. I shall make (him) say: "O Kubaba, you yourself shall make them great in my hand."

§§ 23-31 When he ran to this precinct, I built this seat for him. If this seat shall pass down to any king, who shall take it as a writing surface, whether either he shall take away a stone from these stones, or whether he shall take away a stele for a stele, or who shall erase my name, or who shall take away from these children or from these eunuchs,[114] may the dogs of Nikarawas eat up his head!

2.3.10. KARKAMIŠ A15b

This dedication by Yariris is another building inscription with both historical and religious content. Apart from the usual topoi of such inscriptions, Yariris also includes some interesting information about his own education. If all his claims

---

110. The toponym Sura in Luwian inscriptions clearly refers to more than one place. Its identification in this inscription is uncertain. The author of this inscription, Yariris, spells the city Assur differently in another inscription, which seems to argue against an identification with Assur (cf. KARKAMIŠ A15b § 19). The most recent discussion of the problem is found in Simon, forthcoming, who argues that Sura was the Luwian name for Tabal, and understands the attestations of this clause and KARKAMIŠ A4b § 2 as referring to Tabal.

111. Presumably referring to the sculpture accompanying this inscription.

112. Without understanding the defining terms, the picture this evokes is of people (probably Kamanis's brothers) being granted the positions (with their respective symbols) for which they are destined.

113. The brothers?

114. Hawkins (2000: 125) interprets this passage as "taking away (someone)" from the two groups but I don't think a direct object is necessarily required if one were to understand "take away from" in the sense of "diminish".

are true, he was thoroughly trained in foreign languages and writing systems, presumably to fit the role as close confidant and advisor of the king.

side

1   § 1   EGO-*wa/i-mi-i* ¹*i-ara/i-ri+i-sá* |IUDEX-*ni-sa* (DEUS)TONITRUS-*ta-ti-i* (DEUS)*ku*+AVIS-*pa-pa-ti* (DEUS)*kar-hu-ha-ti-i* (DEUS)SOL-*tà-ti-i-ha* (LITUUS)*á-za-mi-sa* CAPUT-*ti-sá*

     § 2   *wa/i-mu-u kar-ka-mi-sà*(URBS) SUPER+*ra/i-´* PUGNUS(-)*la/i/u-mi* PUGNUS-*ri+i-i-ia-ha i-zi-ia-ta* DEUS-*ni-zi*

     § 3   *a-wa/i kar-ka-mi-sà-na*(URBS) PUGNUS(-)*la/i/u-mi-ha*

     § 4   DOMINUS-*na-ni-ia-za-*[*pa/ha*]-*wa/i-mu* [DOMUS?]-*na-za* [PUGNUS?-*ri*]+*i-ha*

     § 5   *kar-ka-mi-*[*sà*]-*pa*[-*wa/i*(URBS)...

2   ... || ...

     § 6   ...]x[...]-*ha*(-)?

     § 7   ‹*wa/i*›-*ta* FLUMEN-*pi-na* |"PES$_2$"(-)*hi-nu-ha* (X?)*á-ta$_5$/i$_5$*(-)|*sà-na-ha*

     § 8   *wa/i-ta* |*zi-na* FLUMEN-*pi-na* "PES$_2$"(-)*hi-nu-ha*

     § 9 |*zi-ha-wa/i-ta* FLUMEN-*pi-i-na* "PES$_2$"(-)*hi-nú-ha*

     § 10   (DEUS)*hara/i-ma-na-wa/i-na-sa-pa-wa/i*(URBS) DEUS. DOMUS-*tà* AEDIFICARE+*MI-ha*

     § 11   *á-mi-i-na-pa-wa/i*(-)*u!-mu!* ("COR")*á-tara/i-i-na* |"SCALPRUM"(-)*i-ara/i-za i-zi-i-ha*

     § 12   *wa/i-mu-tá* (DEUS)*ku*+AVIS-*pa-pa-sa* |("PES")*pa-ta$_5$/i$_5$-´* PONERE-*mi-i-na* |CAPERE-*i* ||

3   § 13   ¹*ka-ma-ni-na-pa-wa/i-´* CRUS+CRUS(-)*ní-ia-sa-ta-la-na* MAGNUS+*ra/i-nu-ha-´*

     § 14   *wa/i-ta* |REX-*tá-za* |"FRONS"-*hi-ti* *273-*na* |REL-*ti* MANUS.*273(-)*su-hi-i-ti-ha*

     § 15   POST+*ra/i-zi-pa-wa/i-tú* |FRATER.LA-*zi-i* |MAGNUS+*ra/i-nu-ha*

     § 16 |*wa/i-ta* |("INFANS.NI")*á-ta$_5$/i$_5$-la-za* |*a-ta sa-sa-ha*

86   HIEROGLYPHIC LUWIAN INSCRIPTIONS

§ 17 |("CUBITUM")*ka+ra/i-mara/i-ta-hi-sà-pa-wa/i-ma-za-ta á-mi-ia-za-´* |DOMINUS-*na-ni-ia-za* ¹*á-sa-ti-ru-wa/i-sá* |INFANS-*ni-ia-za ARHA* ("LONGUS")*ia+ra/i-i-ha*

§ 18 |*wa/i-mu* DEUS-*ni-zi-´* x x[...

4   ... || ...

§ 19 ...]URBS-*si-ia-ti* |SCRIBA-*li-ia-ti zú+ra/i-wa/i-ni-ti*(URBS) |SCRIBA-*li-ia-ti-i a-sú+ra/i*(REGIO)-*wa/i-na-ti*(URBS) |SCRIBA-*li-ia-ti-i ta-i-ma-ni-ti-ha*(URBS) SCRIBA-*li-ti*

§ 20 12-*ha-wa/i-´* |"LINGUA"-*la-ti-i-na* (LITUUS)*u-ni-ha*

§ 21 |*wa/i-mu-u ta-ni-ma-si-na* REGIO-*ni-si-i-na-´* |INFANS-*ni-na* |("VIA")*ha+ra/i-wa/i-ta-hi-ta₅/i₅-ti-i* CUM-*na ARHA-sa-ta* DOMINUS-*na-ni-i-sa á-mi-i-sa* |"LINGUA"-*la-ti* SUPER+*ra/i-´*

§ 22 *ta-ni-mi-ha-wa/i-mu* (*273)*wa/i+ra/i-pi-na* (LITUUS)*u-na-nu-ta*

top

§ 23 [*z*]*a-pa-wa/i* "SCALPRUM"-*su-na za-ma-ti-i-na-´ wa/i-mi-*LITUUS-*ha*

§ 24 [*wa/i*]-*mu-u* STATUA-*ti u-mu* SUPER?-*ru*-x-x

§ 25 *i-zi?-ia-sa₄?-sà?-ti-pa-wa/i-ta* |REL-*i-sa* |NEG₂-´ LITUUS+*u*-x-*ti-i á?-la?-sa?-i?*

§ 26 |*za-sa-wa/i-´ sà-na*-x-*i*(*a*)?

§ 27 *wa/i-mu-u* [...]-*ti?-sa?*...-*sá* ...

§ 28 x-x-*ta*...*ha-na*...-*wa/i-mu?-ti* x-*sa-ha* "FRONS"-*su?- ta₅/i₅?* x x |*á*-[...]*i*[...

§ 29 ...]*á*... LOCUS-*ta₄/i₄-ti* |"CRUS"-*nu-sà-wa/i-´*

§§ 1–5   I (am) the ruler Yariris, the prince beloved by the Storm God, Kubaba, Karhuha, and the Sun. The gods made me strong and exalted over Karkamiš. I strengthened Karkamiš, [and] I [exal]ted my lord's house(?), and Karkamiš [...]

§§ 6–12 I caused the river to pass ..., I caused the river to pass here, and here, too, I caused the river to pass. I built the temple of the god of Harmana, and I made my own statue ..., and Kubaba will take (it) for me, placed at (her) foot.

§§ 13–18 I brought up Kamanis as successor, wherefore I showed(?) virtue above all kings. And I brought up his younger brothers, I let them in(?)[115] as brothers and I extended protection to them, the children of my lord Astiruwas. The gods [...] me [...

§§ 19–22 ...] in the writing of the city, in the writing of Tyre (Phoenician),[116] in the Assyrian writing and in the Taimani (Aramaic?) writing. And I knew twelve languages. By travelling, my lord raised a son of every country for me regarding language, and he caused me to know every skill.

§§ 23–29 I found this ZAMATI stone, and [I ...ed] for my statue ...

2.3.11. KULULU 1

This building inscription belongs to a group of inscriptions from Tabal. The text is carved into three sides of a small stela. Its author Ruwas identifies himself as a servant of Tuwatis, the father of King Wasusarmas.[117] Although this texts contains a large number of words which we do not understand yet, if compared to the above Karkamiš inscriptions it still illustrates a certain uniformity of Hieroglyphic writing beyond local boundaries.

1	§ 1	|EGO-wa/i-mi ¹ru-wa/i-sa ¹tu-wa/i-ti-i-sá SERVUS-ta_4/i_4-sa
	§ 2	|a-wa/i |za-ia [|]DOMUS-na-´ [? s]a-hi-zi-i |á-sá-ta |ha-ta-ma
	§ 3	|wa/i-tà |ta-ma-ha
	§ 4	|wa/i-tà |DOMUS-na-´ |i-zi-a-ha ||
2	§ 5	|za-ha-wa/i |a+ra/i-ta-la-si-na |(DEUS)TONITRUS-hu-u-za-na-´ |á-mu |ta-nu-wa/i-ha-´
	§ 6	|wa/i-na |("ANNUS")u-si-na |("ANNUS")u-si-na 1 ("BOS.ANIMAL")wa/i-wa/i-ti-i 3 ("OVIS.ANIMAL")ha-wa/i-ti |sa-sa_5+ra/i-la-wa/i
3	§ 7	|wa/i-ti || |za-ia |DOMUS-na-´ |REL-sá |tu-wa/i-ti-ia |wa/i-zi-ti-‹i›
	§ 8	|ni-pa-wa/i |á-ma-ta-´ |ni-pa-wa/i |la-hi?-zi-i |ni-pa-wa/i |wa/i-ia-ni-[si?-]i |tu-wa/i[+ra/i]-sà-za-´
	§ 9	|REL-sà-ha-wa/i-sa |REL-sa-pa

---

115. Meaning not entirely clear. Maybe "admit" to position of power or status?
116. Cf. Yakubovich 2010a: 81 n. 58; Simon, forthcoming.
117. For Ruwas, see inscription KULULU 4, p. 50; for Wasusarmas see inscriptions TOPADA, p. 54, SULTANHAN, p. 98.

	§ 10	|á-pa||-ti-pa-wa/i |a+ra/i-ta-la-si-sá |(DEUS)TONI-TRUS-hu-u-za-sá |á-pa-si-na |a+ra/i-ta-li-na |SUB-ni?-na |ha-pa-za-nu-wa/i-tu-u
4		
	§ 11	¹tu-wa/i-ti-sà-pa-wa/i-tu-u-ta |á-mu+ra/i-sa |(DEUS)ku-AVIS-pa-pa-sa |ha-sa-mi-sa zú-wa/i-ni-i-sá |á-pa-na-´ || i-zi-ia-tu
5		
	§ 12	|a-wa/i |á-pa-si-na |ha-sa-mi-na |mara/i-ta-mi-i-na |ARHA |á-za-tu |á-pa-si-ha |á-tara/i-i-na
	§ 13	¹tu-wa/i-ti-ia-pa-wa/i-ta |za-zi |DEUS-ni-zi-i |wa/i-su |á-wa/i-i-tu
6	§ 14	wa/i-tà || |ni-i |REL-ti-i-ha |pi-i[a]-a-i
	§ 15	|á-mu-pa-wa/i REL-‹i› |DEUS-[n]a-za |ta-wa/i-ia-na |ARHA |i-wa/i ¹tu-wa/i-ti-sa-ti |tara/i-u-na-ti
	§ 16	|za-ia-pa-wa/i DOMUS-na zi-ti

§§ 1–4   I (am) Ruwas, servant of Tuwatis. These houses were ruined for SAHINZI. I built them, and I made them houses.

§§ 5–6   I myself also set up this Storm God of the ARATALI. And I shall sacrifice to him every year one ox (and) three sheep.

§§ 7–10 Who(ever) shall demand these houses for himself from Tuwatis, or the AMATA, or the LAHI(ZI), or the vineyard of vine(s), whosoever he (be), may the Storm God of the ARATALI cause to ... ... his own ARATALI!

§§ 11–16 May the HASAMI dog of Kubaba, the AMURA of Tuwatis make after him! May it eat up his HASAMI MARATAMI and his (own) person! But may these gods come well for Tuwatis, and let him not give it to anyone (else)! But when, by the justice of Tuwatis, I myself shall go away before the gods, these houses (will be) here.

2.4. Dedicatory Inscriptions

The boundary between the literary genres is fluid, some building inscriptions also contain dedications, while dedicatory inscriptions, like the former, may contain historical narratives. Nevertheless, it seems appropriate to group the following inscriptions together in a section of their own.

2.4.1. BABYLON 2 AND BABYLON 3

Among objects found outside of their place of origin are a stele (BABYLON 1) and two stone bowls from Babylon (BABYLON 2; 3) and the lead letters from Assur (ASSUR letters, p. 109). Note that the names of these objects indicate their find spot but not that they were fashioned there. It is thought that the Babylon objects were originally placed before the Storm God at his most important cult center at Aleppo, ancient Halab. The bowl BABYLON 3, restored from several fragments, specifically mentions that it is a dedication to this deity. It is not at all clear how these objects came to Babylon, although the most likely explanation is that they were brought there as booty.

BABYLON 2

§ 1 |*za-ia-wa/i* ("SCALPRUM")*ka-ti-na* SERVUS-*ta$_5$/i$_5$-a-sa* LITUUS+CAELUM-*na* (DEUS)TONITRUS-*ti-i i-zi-i-tà*

§ 2 *wa/i-tu-u* |*wa/i-i* REL-*za* |*sa-há*

§ 3 |*wa/i-mu* AUDIRE-*ti-ta*

§ 4 *á-mu-pa-wa/i-tu* ("*419")*wa/i-sa-ha-i-za ku+ra/i-i-sà(-)ka-tara/i-hi?-ha i-zi-i-ha*

§ 4a |!(DEUS)*ku*+AVIS-*pa-pa-sa* (DEUS)*kar-hu-ha-sa*

§§ 1–4   SERVUS-tas made these bowls for the heavenly Storm God. Because I was woeful(?) to him, he heard me, and I made a consecrated KURI (and) KATARAHI for him, and (of?) Kubaba (and) Karhuha.

BABYLON 3

za-ia-wa/i-´ ("SCALPRUM")*ka-ti-na* CERVUS$_2$-*ti-ia-sa* TONITRUS.*HALPA-pa-ni* (DEUS)TONITRUS-*hu-ti* PRAE-*na* [PON]ERE-*wa/i-ta*

§ 1   Runtiyas placed these bowls before the Halabean Tarhunzas

2.4.2. BABYLON 1

This stela carries a dedication by an unknown ruler Laparizitis to the Storm God of Aleppo, who is depicted on the front of the stela. Laparizitis commissions the stele as a thank offering, yet he does not state which divine favor he is repaying.

Like the two stone bowls found at Babylon, this stela presumably came there as booty, and one may assume that it was originally set up in the temple of the Storm God of Aleppo.

1	§ 1	|EGO-*wa/i-mi-i* ¹*la*-PRAE-VIR?/*la*?-*sa* |("IUDEX")*tara/i-wa/i-ní-sa* |CAPUT-*ti-i-sa*
2	§ 2	*wa/i-mu-ta-*a* TONITRUS.HALPA-*pa-wa/i¹-ní-sa* ||(DEUS)TONITRUS-*sa* |BONUS-*ti-i* |HWI-*ia-ta*
3	§ 3	*wa/i-tu-*a mi-i-na-*a* ¹FEMINA-*ti-i-na* |BONUS-*mi-i-na* |INFANS-*ní-i-na* ¹*á-na-si-na*|| *pi-ia-ha*
	§ 4	|*á-ma-za-pa-wa/i-'* REL-*a-za* |*ta-ní-ma-za*
	§ 5	|*ma-wa/i-sa* |"TERRA"-*si* |"FINES"-*sa*
	§ 6	|*ma-pa-wa/i-sa* |"VITIS"-*si-i* |"FINES"-*sa*
4	§ 7	|*ma-pa*||-*wa/i-sa* |"AEDIFICIUM"-*si-i* |"FINES"-*sa*
	§ 8	REL-*a-za* REL-*i-ta* PES-*i*
	§ 9	*wa/i-tu-tà-*a* TONITRUS.HALPA-*pa-wa/i-ní* (DEUS)TONITRUS-*ti-i* |*pa+ra/i-na-'* |PRAE-*i pi-ia-ha*
5	§ 10	|*a-tá-pa-wa/i-ta* REL-*i-sa*|| |CRUS-*i* |("*471")*á-za-i* |*pa-za-i*
	§ 11	|*ma-pa-wa/i-sa a-tá-ti-li-i-sa* | *ta₄/i₄-la/i/u-ní-sa-*a*
	§ 12	|*ma-pa-wa/i-sa* |ARHA-*ti-i-li-sa* | *ta₄/i₄-la/i/u-ní-sa-*a*
6	§ 13	*za-pa*||-*wa/i-ta* |("STELE")*wa/i-ní-za* |"LOCUS"-*ta₅/i₅-za-'* |(SA₄)*sá-ni-ti-i*
	§ 14	|NEG₂-*pa-wa/i-tà* |ARHA |MALLEUS-*i*
	§ 15	[|*pa*]-*ti-*‹pa›*-wa/i-*a* TONITRUS.HALPA-*pa-wa/i-ní-sa* (DEUS)TONITRUS-*sa* |*ara/i-'* |*pa-ta* |NEG₃-*sa* |*pi-ia-i* || ARHA
7		|DELERE-*nu-u-na*

§§ 1–9   I (am) Laparizitis(?), the prince-ruler. For me the Halabean Storm-God ran with favor (and) to him I gave my dear daughter Anasis as a child. All that (is) mine, whether it (be) the border of a (piece of) land or the border of a vineyard or the border of a building: whatever stands(?) anywhere, before him, the Halabean Storm-God, I handed it over.

§§ 10–15 Who comes inside, eats(?) (and) drinks(?), whether he (be) an inner enemy or an outer enemy or overthrows this stele from its place or erases it: may the Halabean Storm-God not give him ARA PATA to destroy!

2.4.3. TELL AHMAR 6

This dedicatory inscription was commissioned by the ruler Hamiyatas, King of Masuwari (modern Tell Ahmar), who is also the author of several other inscriptions. The text contains a dedication to the Storm God Tarhunzas and a long historical narrative. The text employs a number of standard topoi to illustrate the relationship of the king with his gods—naming an impressive list of gods favoring him—and to contrast his achievements and position with those of his forefathers.

1	§ 1	EGO-wa/i-mi ¹ha-mi-ia-ta-sa |IUDEX-ní-sa |ma-su-wa/i+ra/i-za-<sa>(URBS) |REX-ti-i-sa (DEUS)TONITRUS-si SERVUS-ta₄/i₄-i-sa
	§ 2	wa/i-mu-*a |á-ia-ta₅/i₅-na |INFANS(-)ní-*282-wa/i-ra+a CAELUM (DEUS)TONITRUS-sa (DEUS)ia-[...] (DEUS)BONUS (DEUS)LUNA-sa |á-ta-na |(PES₂)tara/i-za-mi-i-sa (DEUS)SOL-sa (DEUS)CERVUS-sa|
2		(DEUS)kar-hu-ha-sa (DEUS)ku+AVIS (DEUS)hi-pu-tà-sa EXERCITUS-la/i/u-na-si-ha (DEUS)sà-US-ka-sa [(DEUS)]FORTIS-sa (DEUS)SARMA-sa |"CAELUM"-ti-sa |"TERRA"-REL+ra/i-ti-sa-ha (DEUS)AVIS-ti-zi (DEUS)*30(-)tà-ti-zi a-tá |ta-sa²-mi-zi DEUS-ní-zi |(LITUUS)á-za-ta
3	§ 3	wa/i-mu-*a|á-ma-za |tá-ti-ia-za |"LIGNUM"-la-ha-za || |pi-ia-ta
	§ 4	a-wa/i |ku-ma-na mi-i-sa-*a |tá-ti-sa |ha-IUDEX-<+ra/i²>-i-sa sa-tá-*a
	§ 5	|mu-pa-wa/i -*a mi-[i-]zi-*a |tá-ti-zi ta₄/i₄-ní-zi-*a (DEUS.ORIENS)ki-sà-ta-ma-si-zi (DEUS.ORIENS)ki-sà-ta-ma-ti |ARHA |"DELERE"-nú-[sà]-ha
	§ 6	[...]-wa/i |(OCCIDENS)i-pa-ma-si-zi |ARHA |DELERE-nu-sà-ha mi-ia-ti-*a|DOMINUS-na-ní-ia-ti |*314-sa-ta-na-ti
4	§ 7	|PRAE-pa-wa/i||-mu |za-a-sa |EXERCITUS-la/i/u-na-si-sa (DEUS)TONITRUS-sa |hu-ha-sà-ta-si
	§ 8	|REL-ia-pa-wa/i mi-i-sa-*a |tá-ti-sa |ARHA (MORI)wa/i-la-tá

§ 9 [za-a-zi]-pa-wa/i-mu DEUS-ní-zi |(MANUS)su-hi-tà |(LITUUS)á-za-ta

§ 10 a-wa/i mi-ia-za-*a |tá-ti-ia-za |á-ta₅/i₅-ma-za |NEG₂-´ |INFRA-ta LITUUS?+na?-tà(?)

§ 11 |SUPER+ra/i-a-ha-wa/i |na?-ní-tà

§ 12 DEUS-na-za-pa-wa/i |VIA-wa/i-na |(LITUUS)tara/i-wa/i-i-ha

§ 13 wa/i-ma-za-ta-*a |(MANUS)su-za |(*314)ha-zi-wa/i-sà PONERE-wa/i∥-ha

§ 14 |CAPUT-ti-pa-wa/i |INFANS-ní-i |COR-tara/i-na |BONUS-li-ia-nu-wa/i-ha |("CAPUT")ha+ra/i-ma-hi-na

§ 15 |*187-wa/i-sa-pa-wa/i-ta |1-ta-ti-i |(PES₂)tara/i-zi-ha

§ 16 |FINES-hi-zi-pa-wa/i |za-la-na |PONERE-wa/i-ha

§ 17 |za-a-sa-pa-wa/i-mu |EXERCITUS-la/i/u-na-si-i-sa (DEUS)TONITRUS-sa |(LITUUS)á-za-ta

§ 18 wa/i-ma-sa-*a |LITUUS?+na?-hi-i-tà |VIA(-)hu-sa-la-hi-tà-ha wa/i+ra/i-li-ta

§ 19 wa/i-ma-sa-*a |PRAE-na |hu-ha-sà-ta-si

§ 20 a-wa/i |FINES-hi-zi |("COR")la-tara/i-ha ∥

§ 21 ta₄/i₄-ni-zi-pa-wa/i-mi-i-*a |ARHA |("DELERE")mara/i-nu-wa/i-ha

§ 22 wa/i-mu-*a DEUS-na-mi-i-sa |á-sa₅-za-ta

§ 23 |EXERCITUS-la/i/u-na-si-i-wa/i (DEUS)TONITRUS-na (SOLIUM)i-sà-nu-wa/i

§ 24 |a-wa/i |REL-a-ti-i |(ANNUS)u-si-i |FLUMEN *427.*311-pa-x |(PES₂)i-ha (DEUS)TONITRUS-sa-ti |(*314)ha-sa-ta-na-ti-i 5 x CENTUM(-)ta-na-ti |("SCALA+PES+ROTA")za-la-la-ti-i |*179.*347.5(-)ia-ma-ti |*187(-)REL-ta-na-ti-i-ha-wa/i ∥ EXERCITUS-la/i/u-na-ti-i

§ 25 |ARHA-pa-wa/i |REL-i |PES-wa/i-i-ha

§ 26 a-wa/i |za-a-na |EXERCITUS-la/i/u-na-si-na (DEUS)TONITRUS-na pa-ti-i-*a |(ANNUS)u-si-i |(SOLIUM)i-sà-nu-wa/i-ha

TEXTS

§ 27   *a-wa/i* |REL-*ia* | *527(-)*na-ta-ti-i* |(CURRUS)*wa/i+ra/i-za-ní-i-sa* |(SA₄)*sá-za-i*

§ 28 |*za-a-ti-pa-wa/i* |EXERCITUS-*la/i/u-na-sa-na* (DEUS)TONITRUS-*ti-i* |9 BOS-*za* |*pi-pi-sa-wa/i*

§ 29   ¹*ha-mi-i-ia-ta-sa-pa-wa/i-ta* |*á-ta₅/i₅-ma-za* |REL-*i-sa* |ARHA |"MALLEUS"(-) AVIS-*la-i* ||

8   § 30 |NEG₂-*a-pa-wa/i* ¹*ha-mi-ia-ta-sa-na* |NEPOS-*sa-ta-ní-i* |REL-*i-sa* |MALUS-*wa/i-za-´* |POST-*ni a-tá* |(COR.ANIMAL) *za+ra/i-ti-ti-i*

§ 31   *pa-ti-pa-wa/i-*a* |*za-sa* |EXERCITUS-*la/i/u-na-si-i-sa* (DEUS)TONITRUS-*sa* |LEO(ANIMAL)-*wa/i-sa* |*i-zi-ia-ru*

§ 32   *a-wa/i pa-si-na-*a* |(CAPUT)*ha+ra/i-ma-hi-na* FEMINA-*ti-i-na* |INFANS-*ni-na* |INFRA-*ta* |(BIBERE)*pa-sà-tú*

§ 33   *wa/i-tú-ta-*a* LOCUS-*ta₄/i₄-wa/i-za* |NEG₃-*sa* CUM *u-sa-la-li-ti*

§ 34 |*á-na*(REGIO)-*i-ta-pa-wa/i* NEG₃-*sa-a-pa* |(PES₂)*i-ti* |*za-a-na* (DEUS)TONITRUS-*na* ¹*ha-mi-ia-ta-si-i-na* |*wa/i+ra/i-*273-na*

§ 1   I am the ruler Hamiyatas, king of Masuwari, servant of the Storm God.

§§ 2–3   And they loved me, the first-born[118] child: the heavenly Storm God, Ea, the Grain God, the Moon God, the affectionate[119] Sun God, Runtiya, Karhuha, Kubaba, Hepat, and Šauška of the Army, Teššub, Šarruma, Heaven and Earth, the ... Gods,[120] the ... Gods,[121] the ANDA TASAMINZI Gods. And they granted me my paternal succession.

§§ 4–7   When my father was alive,[122] I destroyed my father's enemies, the ones of the east towards the east, the ones of the west I destroyed with the help of my Lord. And this Storm God of the Army ran before me.

---

118. For *ayala-* "first born" see Rieken and Yakubovich 2010: 212.
119. *anda tarzamis*: inclined (towards me), thus affectionate; cf. Rieken 2004: 459.
120. AVIS-*tinzi*: unknown.
121. *30-tatinzi*: unknown.
122. *ha*-IUDEX<+*ra/i?*>-*i-sa*: note the rebus writing within the word, using IUDEX to write /*tarwani*/ in *hatar-wani-*, "alive."

§§ 8–11   But when my father died, these gods loved me abundantly. They did not look(?) down on the name of my father, and they ...ed (it) up.

§§ 12–16   I provided(?)[123] the way for the gods, and I established a full ritual for them. For the man (and) the boy, I raised person and head. I turned ...[124] the *187. And I closed(?)[125] the borders.

§§ 17–21   But this Storm God of the Army loved me ...[126] He ran before me and I extended the frontiers, and I myself destroyed the enemies.

§§ 22–28   And one belonging to the god spoke to me: Cause the Storm God of the Army to dwell (here)! And in that year I went ... with the help of the Storm God with 500 carriages, with ... and with the ... army. When I came out (returned?), in that year I settled the Storm God of the Army. ... and the war chariot will ... And I shall always give nine oxen to this Storm God of the Army.

§§ 29–34   But who(soever) shall delete the name of Hamiyatas, or who desires evil for the descendants of Hamiyatas, for him may this Storm God of the Army become a lion! May he swallow down his head, his wife (and) child! With him may he not USALALI the ..., nor let him go to the country Anaita to ... this Storm God of Hamiyatas!

2.4.4. ALEPPO 2

This text is a dedicatory inscription by an individual called Arpas to his "lord and brother" Hamiyatas, ruler of Tell Ahmar, the author of the previous inscription. Nothing further is known about the identity of Arpas, who only identifies himself as a servant of the Storm God. Is he a member of Hamiyatas family, maybe even a brother in the literal sense of the word? Or could he be a member of the other, competing family line, posing a challenge to the legitimacy of Hamiyatas's rule? Might he even be the son of Ariyahinas, whose name is not preserved?

1   § 1   EGO-mi-i ^{1}ara/i-pa-sa (DEUS)TONITRUS-si |BONUS-mi-i-sa SERVUS-ta_4/i_4-i-sa

    § 2   wa/i-mu-*a CAELUM (DEUS)TONITRUS-sa ha+ra/i-na-
2   wa/i-ni-sa(URBS) (DEUS)LUNA+MI-sa |x x ||[...] x-x-ta

---

123. See Hawkins 2006: 23–24.
124. 1-tati seems to be an adverb related to the numeral one. Once?
125. Lit. put the borders ZALAN; cf. Hawkins 2006: 25–26.
126. Another rather obscure clause follows.

§ 3 wa/i-mu-*a mi-i-sa-*a DOMINUS-na-ni-sa |FRATER.LA-i-sa-ha |X+RA/I-ti REL?-ta

§ 4 |za-a-zi-pa-wa/i-mu DEUS-ni-zi |REX-‹tá?›-hi-tà CUM-ni |PES$_2$.PES$_2$-tà-ti-i

§ 5 ‹wa/i›-mu-*a |x-x-ia |(BESTIA)HWI-sà+ra/i-sa

§ 6 wa/i-ta |PRAE-na ARHA |(PUGNUS+PUGNUS)hu-hu+ra/i-pa-ti-i

§ 7 mu-pa-wa/i-*a |URBS-ni-zi-´ NEG$_2$-´ [... || ...]

§ 8 wa/i-mi-*a (DEUS)SOL-ni-za ("LIGNUM")ta-ru-sa |i-zi-i-ha(-)si

§ 9 a-wa/i mi-na-´ |FRATER.LA-na ¹ha-mi-i[a]-ta-NEG$_2$ NEG$_2$-´ |[...]-ha

§ 10 a-wa/i pa-sa-*a |á-ta$_5$/i$_5$-ma-za (DEUS)TONITRUS CUM-ni |PONERE-wa/i-‹ha›

§ 11 |"COR"-tara/i-pa-wa/i-na NEG$_2$-´ |REL-i-ha a-tá |CRUS+RA/I-nu-wa/i-ha

§ 12 mu-pa-wa/i‹-*a x›-sa zi-i-x-x || |BONUS-sa$_5$+ra/i-ti |DARE-tá

§ 13 |ARHA-pa-wa/i-ta |REL-sa |CAPERE-i

§ 14 pa-pa-wa/i-*a CAELUM (DEUS)TONITRUS ha+ra/i-na-wa/i-ni-sa(URBS)-ha (DEUS)LUNA+MI-sa |(LOQUI)tá-tara/i-ia-tú

§ 15 wa/i-tú-*a |CAELUM[... ...] |ni-i INFRA-tá |PES-wa/i-ti-i

§ 16 |("TERRA")ta-sà-REL+ra/i-ti-pa-wa/i-ta |("*471")(m)u?-ru-wa/i-tà-za |ní-i |SUPER+ra/i-´ |PES-wa/i-ti

§ 17 mi-i-pa-wa/i-*a |FRATER(-)x||[...]x |REL-a-za |BONUS-sa$_5$+ra/i-ti-i |pi-pa-sa-wa/i-i

§ 18 |ARHA-pa-wa/i-tú-wa/i-tà-ta |REL-sa |CAPERE-i

§ 19 |ma-wa/i-tú-wa/i-sa |tá-ti-sa

§ 20 |ma-pa-wa/i-sa |*274 [...]

§ 21 pa-ti-pa-wa/i-ta-*a |za-a-zi DEUS-ni-zi |LIS-la/i/u-sa-tú

§ 22 wa/i-tú-*a |á-ta$_5$/i$_5$-ma-za |ARHA |"DELERE"-tú

6	§ 23	|ha+ra/i-na-wa/i-ni-pa-w[a/i... || ...]-ia-ti FEMINA-ti-ia-ti |X-zi á-pa-si-z[i] |AR[HA] |(FLAMMAE(?))ki-[n]ú-sà-tú
	§ 24	|za-ti-pa-wa/i DEUS-ni-i |REL-sa |MALUS-ta_4/i_4-a-ti |VERSUS-ia-na |PES-wa/i-ti-i
	§ 25	NEG$_2$-pa-wa/i ¹ara/i-pa-ia |REL-sa |("CORNU")tara/i-pa |CRUS-i
	§ 26	pa-pa-wa/i-*a (DEUS)ku+A[VIS ...] (DEUS) [i]-ia-[...

§ 1   I (am) Arpas, beloved servant of the Storm God.

§§ 2–7   The Storm God of Heaven and the Moon God of Harran [ran] before me. Where(?) my lord and brother shall ... (for) me, these gods shall walk with me for kingship. And for me the ... (shall be) wild beasts, they shall PARAN ARHA HUHURPA (them). And the cities did not [...] me.

§§ 8–12   I made a statue of the Sun God for myself. I did not [...] my brother Hamiyatas. And I established his name with the Storm God. But I did not set him up (as) a figure, and he gave ... to me with goodness.

§§ 13–16   But whoever takes it/them away, may the Storm God of Heaven and the Moon God of Harran curse him! Let [the ...] not come down from heaven for him, and let the seed(?) not come up from the earth.[127]

§§ 17–22   What I always give to my brother in goodness, whosoever shall take it away from him, whether he (be) a father to him, or whether he (be) a *274[...],[128] may the gods prosecute him, may they destroy his name!

§§ 23–26   For the [Moon God of]Harran, for [ma]le (and) female let his/their ... burn up. But who(soever) comes towards this god with malice, or who(soever) stands for trampling on Arpas, [may] Kubaba and Ea [...] him!

2.4.5. BOHÇA

Bohça is located in the southeast of the Anatolian plateau, ancient Tabal. On this stele, the ruler Kurtis, son of Ashwis, records a dedication to two gods, the Storm God Tarhunzas and the Stag God Runtiyas. The author is quite possibly identical with Kurti of (A)tun(n)a, attested in Assyrian annals for the years 718 and 713 B.C.E.

---

127. Let it not rain and let nothing grow?

128. The second of this pair of offenders, unfortunately, only preserves the determinative *274.

TEXTS

The main subject of the inscription is hunting, but as the text breaks off after the fourth line, it is difficult to judge whether the stele was set up to mark Kurtis's hunting territory, or whether the topic of hunting was used as an image of a royal pursuit, to display manliness in times of peace. Further, the author demonstrates Kurtis's relationship with his two personal deities, and uses typical imagery known from many other inscriptions. The text relies heavily on standard formulae and repetition.

1	§ 1	EGO-*mi* [|?]*ku+ra/i-ti-i-sa* |*á-‹sa-*HWI-*si›-sa*$_4$ |HEROS-*li-i-sa* |("INFANS")*ni-mu-wa/i-za-sa* ("OCCIDENS")*i-pa-ma-ri+i-i* |ORIENS+*MI-ma-ri+i-ha* |PRAE |AUDIRE+*MI-ti-mi-‹sa*$_4$› ‖ [|]
2		REX-*ti-sá*
	§ 2	|*wa/i-ta* |(DEUS)TONITRUS-*hu-ti* |*za-ri+i* |(BONUS)*wa/i-su-wa/i-i*
	§ 3	|*wa/i-mu* |TERRA-REL+*ra/i-zi* |SUPER+*ra/i* |"CAPERE"(-)*la/i/u-na-´* |*pi-pa-sa-i*
	§ 4	|(DEUS)CERVUS$_2$-*ti-pa-wa/i-ta-´* |*za-ri+i*(-)*ia*(-)*pa-´* |(BONUS)*wa/i-su-wa/i*
3	§ 5	|*wa/i-mu* |*za-ri+i* |*sà-ma-ia* ‖ ("ANIMAL.BESTIA")HWI-*sa*$_5$+*ra/i* |*pi-pa-sa-ia*
	§ 6	|*á-mi-zi-pa-wa/i* |*tá-ti-zi-i* |AVUS-*ha-zi-ha* |REL-*zi* [|?]*sa-ta*
	§ 7	|REL-*pa-wa/i* (DEUS)TONITRUS-*hu-za-sa* |NEG$_2$ |REL-*ha-na* |*wa/i+ra/i-ia-ia*
	§ 8	|*á-mu-wa/i* |REL+*ra/i* |*wa/i+ra/i-ia-ia*
	§ 9	|*wa/i-mu* |"TERRA"-REL+*ra/i-zi* SUPER+*ra/i* |"CAPERE"(-)*la/i/u-na* |*pi-pa-sa-ia*
4	§ 10	|*á-mi-zi-ha‹-wa/i›* |*tá-ti-zi* ‖ AVUS-*ha-zi-ha-´?* |REL-*i* "ANIMAL.EQUUS‹">-*zú-sà-ta-la-u-na* REL "PES$_2$.PES$_2$"-*tà-ta*
	§ 11	|REL-*pa-wa/i* (DEUS)CERVUS$_2$-*ti-ia-‹sá?›* [|?]NEG$_2$-´ [|?]REL-*ha-na* [|?]*wa/i+ra/i*[-*ia?*]-*ta*
	§ 12	[|?]*á-mu-wa/i* |REL+*ra/i* |*wa/i+ra/i-ia-ia*
	§ 13	|‹*a?*›-*wa/i* |*za-ti-i* |"TERRA"-*sa*-REL+*ra/i-i* |*za-ti-i* |LOCUS-*ta*$_5$/*i*$_5$-*ti-i* 1 CENTUM (ANIMAL)GAZELLA *la-ha* "UNUS?"-*ta* |REL-*za*

§§ 1–5   I (am) Kurtis, the hero Ashwis' son, the king heard of in the west and in the east. And here I am good to the Storm God, and he grants me to take over the territories. But here I am good to Runtiyas (the Stag God), and here he gives me wild animals en masse(?).

§§ 6–12 And (those) who were my fathers and grandfathers, indeed Tarhunzas did not help (them) at all, as he helps me: he grants me to take over the territories. And when my fathers and grandfathers went riding sometime(?), indeed Runtiyas did not help (them) at all, as he helps me.

§ 13   And in this territory, in this place I took 100 gazelles at one time(?) since(?)...

2.4.6. SULTANHAN

This large stela carries a long inscriptions by Sarwatiwaras, a vassal of Wasusarmas.[129] It is dedicated to the Storm God of the Vineyard. This inscription offers a rare insight into ancient agriculture, not normally a topic of stone inscriptions. Nonetheless, this is primarily a religious text, specifying sacrifices to the god and relating his past favors to the author.

(stele, sides)

1   § 1   EGO-*mi-i* [*sa₅+ra/i-wa/i-ti*|-‹*wa/i+ra/i*›-[*sa* ...]-*wa/i*-[...] |INFANS-*ni-sa* |*wa/i-su*-SARMA-*ma-sá-´* |HEROS-*li-i-sá* SERVUS-*ta₅/i₅-sa*

    § 2 |*a-wa/i* |*za-a-na* |(DEUS)TONITRUS-*hu-zá-na* |*tu-wa/i+ra/i-sà-si-i-na* |*ta-nu-wa/i-ha* ‖

2   § 3 |*a-wa/i-sa* |*á-pi-i* |CRUS-*nú-wa/i-mi-i-na* |BOS(ANIMAL)-*ri+i-i* 9 OVIS *a+ra/i-ma-sa-ri+i-i*

    § 4 |*a-wa/i-na* |*u-pa-ha* |HWI-*i*

    § 5 |*wa/i-sá* |OMNIS-*mi-ri+i* [|*sa*]-*na-wa/i-sa-tara/i-ri+i* |*á-wa/i-tà-´*

    § 6 |*wa/i-ti-i* |*mara/i-wa/i-li-sá-´* [|]("PES")*pa-tà* |ARHA-´ |*la+ra/i-ta*

3   § 7 |("VITIS")*wa/i-ia-ni-sa-pa-wa/i-´* |*za-ri+i* ‖ |*sa-na-wa/i-ia-ta-´*

---

129. For the latter, see TOPADA, p. 54.

TEXTS

§ 8 |a-wa/i |tu-wa/i+ra/i-sà-sa |(DEUS)TONITRUS-hu-za-sa ‹|wa/i›-su-SARMA-ma-[ia? ...]-´[...]-ti-i [|mu-w]a/i-ta-li-na-´ |wa/i+ra/i-pi-na |pi-ia-ta

§ 9 |wa/i-tu-u |á-ru-ni-i-zi |á-pa-si-i-zi |("PES")pa+ra/i-za |SUB-na-na |tu-wa/i-ta

§ 10 |ta-nu-wa/i-ha-wa/i-na |REL-i

§ 11 |REL-i-pa-wa/i |(TERRA)ta-sà-REL+ra/i |2 "OVIS"-sa 80 "HORDEUM" CRUS+RA/I ||

4 § 12 |wa/i-na-´ |á-pi-i |zi-na |"AVIS"(-)ta-wa/i-na-ri+i |("PES") u-pa-ha

§ 13 |HWI-pa-wa/i |sa₅+ra/i-wa/i-ti-wa/i+ra/i-ia-´ |wa/i-su-SARMA-ma-sa SERVUS-ta₅/i₅-i |TONITRUS-hu-za-sa |za-a-zi |wa/i+ra/i-ia-zi-´ |CUM-ni |á-tà-´

§ 14 |wa/i-ta |("CAELUM")ti-pa-sa-ri+i |ma-na-wa/i(-)su-na-tà |INFRA-ta |"PES"-wa/i+ra/i

§ 15 |("TERRA")ta-sà-REL+ra/i-ri+i-pa-wa/i-ta-´ mara/i-wa/i-li-sá |SUPER+ra/i-´ |"PES"₂-tà-i |wa/i-ia-ni-sá-ha||

5 § 16 a-wa/i-´ |HWI-sá |MAGNUS+ra/i-ia-ri+i |ma-sa-ti-tà-ia-ri+i-ha

§ 17 |wa/i-ti-i |REL-sa |za-na |DEUS-ni-na |REL-sà-i

§ 18 |wa/i-ta |á-pa-sa-ha |á-pa-sa-za |sa-na-wa/i-ia-za |za-ri+i |a-ta |LITUUS.LITUUS-na-i

§ 19 |REL-sa-pa-wa/i-ta |SUPER+ra/i-ha-´ |PUGNUS-ri+i-ti-i-´

§ 20 |ni-pa-wa/i-ta |ARHA |pa-sà-REL-i

§ 21 |wa/i-tu-u |DEUS-ni-i-zi |MALUS-tà-ti-i |tara/i-pi-wa/i |CRUS-i-´

6 § 22 |a-wa/i |TONITRUS-hu-za-sa |za-´ |tu-wa/i+ra/i-sà-zá || |ma-sa-ha-ni-i-ti

§ 23 |a-wa/i |wa/i-ia-ni-i-sa |PUGNUS-ri+i-ti-i

§ 24 |tara/i-sa-zi-pa-wa/i |ia+ra/i-ti-i

§ 25 |a-wa/i |MILLE ti-wa/i-ta-li-na |á-ia-ti-i

§ 26 |wa/i-tu-u |BOS(ANIMAL)-sa 9 CENTUM-ha ma-tu-sà

§ 27 |POST+ra/i-ta-pa-wa/i a-ta |sa₅+ra/i-wa/i-ia

	§ 28	wa/i-tu-u-ta |ti-na-ta-za |POST+ra/i-ta
	§ 29	|u-sa-li-pa-wa/i-tu-u |2 OVIS(ANIMAL)-zi

(base, sides)

[side A, missing ...]

B	§ 30	[i]-sà-[t]ara/i-la-ti-pa-wa/i-ta-´ |SUPER+ra/i |"PES"-wa/i+ra/i
C	§ 31	|"LUNA"-ma-sá-pa-wa/i-na |ha+ra/i-na-wa/i-ni-sá || |á-pa-sá |("CORNU")ki-pu-tà-´ |a-ta |tu-wa/i-i-´
	§ 32	|REL-i-pa-wa/i-na |ka+ra/i-mi-si-za-sa |(DEUS)ku-AVIS-pa-pa-sa |á-pa-na |mu-wa/i-i
	§ 33 a	|á-ta-ha-si-zi-pa-wa/i-na |DEUS-ni-i-zi |ARHA |á-tà-tu-u ||
D	§ 33b	("CAELUM")ti-pa-sa-si-zi-pa-wa/i-na |DEUS-ni-zi |("TERRA")ta-sà-REL+ra/i-si-zi-ha |VIR-ti-zi |FEMINA-ti-zi-ha
	§ 34	|a-wa/i |za-ti-i |tu-wa/i+ra/i-si-i |MALUS-za |REL-sa |á-pa+ra/i-ta |á-sa₅-za-i
	§ 35	|a-wa/i REL-i |ara/i-[...

(stele, top)

E1	§ 36	|a-ta-pa-wa/i-na |ni-i-i |ma-ru-ha |pa-nu-wa/i-i |TONITRUS-hu-za-sa |tu-wa/i+ra/i-sa
	§ 37	|REL-pa-wa/i |sa₅+ra/i-wa/i-ti-wa/i+r[a/i]-i[a ... || ...]
2	§ 38	‹ni-pa-wa/i›-ta |URBS+MI-ni |HWI-sa-ha-´ |ka-ti-i |CRUS-i
	§ 39	|ni-pa-wa/i-ta |("TERRA")ta-ka-mi-i |HWI-sa-ha |ka-ti-i |ta-i ||

(base, top)

F1	§ 40	|ni-pa-wa/i-ta |wa/i-na |REL-sa-ha |ka-ti-i |CRUS-i
	§ 41	|á-pi-i-wa/i-tà-´ |REX-ti-ia-ri+i |LEPUS+ra/i-ia-ti-i |i-zi-ia-mi-na-´
	§ 42	|a-wa/i |ka-ti-i-sa |ni-i |á-sa-tu-u-´

	§ 43	|a-wa/i-´ |REL-sá |REL-sá |za |LOCUS-ta$_5$/i$_5$-za |PUGNUS.PUGNUS-i-ta||
2	§ 44	|wa/i-tà |NEG$_2$-´ |HWI-sa-ha |mu-wa/i-ta
	§ 45	|a-wa/i-tà |á-pi-i |sa$_5$+ra/i-wa/i-ti-wa/i+ra/i-sá |á-tà |wa/i-su-SARMA-ma-sa-a-ri+i |wa/i+ra/i-ia-ri+i |sa-na-wa/i-sa-tara/i-ri+i-ha
	§ 46	|za-pa-wa/i |a+ra/i-ma-za |REL-sa-´ |za+ra/i-ti-ti-i-i||
3	§ 47	|ni-pa-wa/i-ta-´ |"FEMINA"-na-ti-i-sa |ta-*375-li-i-sa |pa+ra/i(-)sa$_5$+ra/i |u-pa-i
	§ 48	|ni-pa-wa/i-sa-´ LEPUS+ra/i-ia-li-sa
4	§ 49	|ni-pa-wa/i |REX-[...]
	§ 50	|á-pa-[...] |ha-[...]i[... ...
5	§ 51	[ ]-sa-ri+i [...] |tu-pi-ri+i [...]sa[...]ta

§§ 1–3   I (am) [Sarwatiwaras, ...'s] son, servant of the hero Wasusarmas. I set up this Storm God of the Vineyard, (saying): "He is to be set up again with an ox and nine monthling sheep."

§§ 4–9   When I sacrificed to him, he came with all goodness, and at (his) foot the corn stems thrived, and the vine was good here. And the Storm God of the Vineyard gave [to ki]ng Wasusarmas a mighty courage, he put his enemies under his feet.

§§ 10–15   When I set him up, indeed in the land 2 sheep stood (for) 80 (measures of) barley, and I rededicated him with this TAWANI.[130] So the Storm God gave such help[131] to Sarwatiwaras, servant of Wasusarmas, and abundant(?) outpourings(?) will come down from the sky, and the corn stems will come up from the earth, and the vine.

§§ 16–21   Who(ever) shall be great and shall MASTITAYA,[132] and who(ever) shall fear this god, he shall also observe his advantages here. But who(ever) shall rise above (too high?), or shall neglect (him), the gods shall stand for trampling him with malice.

§§ 22–29   The Storm God shall make this vineyard grow: the vine shall grow, it shall spread shoots, and they shall make 1000 (measures of) wine. And (there shall be) to him 9 oxen and 100 (measures of) wine. But

---

130. On AVIS(-)tawani- see Goedegebuure 2007: 324.
131. Lit., these assistances.
132. Hapax legomenon.

thereafter it will increase(?), and in future (there shall be) to him a tithe, and (as) annual (sacrifices there shall be) to him 2 sheep. [...

§§ 30–33 ...] and he shall come up from his seat, and the Moon God of Harran shall put his hooves on him,[133] and Kubaba of Kar(ka)miš shall attack him afterwards. May the gods of the ATAHA eat him up, the gods of the sky and of the earth, male and female!

§§ 34–42 Who(ever) shall hereafter speak evil against this vineyard, and ... [...] May the Storm God not grant him a portion at all in this vineyard. Against Sarwatiwaras [...], or (if) anyone stands for damage for the city, or (if) anyone stands for damage for the land, or (if) anyone stands for damage for the vine, he shall be requited by royal authority: let there be no damage!

§§ 43–51 Whosoever has ...ed this place, no one has mastered(?) it, but Sarwatiwaras has remade it, with the help and goodness of Wasusarmas. Who(ever) desires this name(?), or (if) a ... woman brings it away(?), or (if) he (is) a governor, or a king, ... [...] shall smite with [...].

2.5. Miscellanea

The following texts do not fall neatly into any of the above categories but are too interesting to be omitted.

2.5.1. TELL AHMAR 1

This partly damaged inscription reiterates the story of the ancestral house of a king whose name, unfortunately, is not preserved. The undamaged part of the introduction identifies him as son of Ariyahina, grand-son of Hapatila. He is the last-known Luwian king among the rulers of Tell Ahmar. As mentioned above, these stem from two rival lines of one family. The dynasty began under the author's great-grandfather Hapatilas and father Ariyahinas, before switching to the usurping family line of Hamiyatas, which supplied three rulers (Hamiyatas's father, Hamiyatas, his son). This internal power struggle find its culmination when the son of Ariyahinas claims his birth right back from the son of Hamiyatas, as related in this inscription. It is most interesting that the author appears to judge the reign of Hamiyatas in a favorable light.

---

133. Cf. Yakubovich 2002: 206-7. An alternative interpretation is offered by Hawkins (2000: 466), who translates "horn" instead of "hooves."

TEXTS

The inscription follows the pattern of building and dedicatory inscriptions, yet neither building activity nor dedication are mentioned, the preserved part consists entirely of a historical narrative. If it had purely historical content, it would be a singular inscription within the surviving text corpus.

1 § 1 [EGO ...PN, titles, ...-s]á-ia-mi-i-sá REGIO |REX-ti-i-sa ¹ha-pa-ti-la-si-i-sa |(INFANS.NEPO[S)ha-ma-su-k]a-[l]a-[sa] ¹ara/i-ia-hi-na-si-i-sa |("IUDEX")tara/i-wa/i-ni-sa |(INFANS) ni-mu-wa/i-i-za-sa

2 § 2 wa/i-mu-*a |á-ia-ta$_5$/i$_5$-na |INFANS(-)ni-wa/i-ra+a-*282 |"CAELUM"-si-i-sa || (DEUS)TONI-TRUS-hu-sa (DEUS)i-ia-sa |REX-ti-i-sá (DEUS.BONUS) ku-mara/i-ma-sa$_5$ |(DEUS)"HORDEUM"(-)ma-ti-la/i/u-sa (DEUS)FORTIS-su-pa-sa |ha+ra/i-na-wa/i-ní-i-sa-ha(URBS) (DEUS)LUNA+MI-sa [...](DEUS)k[u+AV]IS-pa-[pa]-sa-ha x-x-si |á-[...]-ha? [...]-mu-ti-sa [...]-sa [...

§ 3 [... ...]x x x (LITUUS)á-za-ta

3 § 4 wa/i-mu-*a |á-ma-za |tá-ti-ia-za |("LIGNUM<">)||s[à-la-h]a-za |pi-ia-t[a]

§ 5a a-[wa/i] (FINES)i+ra/i-[ha]-z[a/i...] |pa-[...]-x

§ 5b [... ma-s]u-wa/i+ra/i-[...C]RUS(‹URBS›) [(CAELUM) ti]-pa-si-i [SUP]ER+ra/i pa+ra/i [...]-‹i›-ha |("CAPUT") ha+ra/i-ma-hi-na

§ 6 ‹"X"›-tú-sa-pa-wa/i-tá |1-ti-i |(PES$_2$)tara/i-zi-ha

§ 7 a-wa/i |ku-ma-na [mi-(i-)s]a-*a [(AVUS)]hu-ha-[...]-sa [REX-ti]-i-sá [sa-tá]-*a

§ 8 [wa/i-sa]-*a pa-[sa]-na-*a |(*274)u-pa-ti-ti |DOMINUS-na-ni-i-sa sa-tá-*a

4 § 9 a-wa/i |("OCCIDENS")i-pa-||ma-ti-i (DEUS.ORIENS.MI)ki-sà-ta-ma-ti-ha |(LIGNUM)ta$_6$-LEPUS+ra/i-ta

§ 10 |á-na(REGIO)-pa-wa/i-sa |REL-i |ARHA ("MORI")wa/i-la-tá

§ 11 mi-pa-wa/i-*a tá-ti-na[-´ REL(?)]-za pa-si-*a |20-tá-ti-i-sa |INFANS-ni-i-na |SUB-na-na |LITUUS+na-tà-´

§ 12 pa-s[a]-wa/i-*a ("LIGNUM")sà-la-ha-za |("*314")ha-CRUS-sá-tara/i-ti |SUPER+ra/i-´ |CAPERE-ta

§ 13   wa/i-tà-*a |zi-la pa-si-*a |(INFANS)ni-mu-wa/i-za-sa ¹ha-mi-ia-ta-sa |PUGNUS-‹ri+i›-ta

§ 14   wa/i-mu-*a mi-i-*a (AVUS)hu-ha-ti |LIGNUM-la-ha-ti |SUPER+ra/i-´ x-x-ta ||

§ 15   [...]x[...]tá pa[...]pa-s[á?]-*a "DOMUS"-[...] |"DOMINUS"-na[-ni?]-i-na |i-zi-i-tà

§ 16   pa-sa-za-‹pa?›-wa/i-mu-*a |FRATER.LA-za |MAGNUS+ra/i-za-na |i-zi-i-tà

§ 17   wa/i-mu-*a |CRUS-ni-‹mi›-i-sa |("FRONS")ha-ta-za |SUB-na-na |"LITUUS+PA"-za-la-ní-ta

§ 18   [ARHA]-‹pa-wa/i›-sá |REL-i ("MORI")wa/i-la-tá

§ 19   wa/i-mu-*a pa-si-i-*a |(INFANS)ni-mu-wa/i-i-za-sa MALUS-wa/i-z[a]-´ |CUM-ni |("LIGNUM")LEPUS+ra/i-ia-ta

§ 20   mi-i-ha-wa/i-*a |(*274)u-pa-ti-ti-i |("MALUS₂")ha-ha-ní-wa/i-||z[a-´] |CU[M-ni] |(["]COR["])z[a]+ra/i-ti-i-ta

§ 21   m[u]-pa-wa/i-´*a|za-‹a›-ti-i-´ "‹CAELUM›"-sa-na [(DEUS)]TONITRUS-hu-ti |(‹MANUS›)i-s[a-tara/i]-x |SUPER[+ra/i-´] |[...

§ 22   wa/i-tú-*a |á-[...] mara/i-[...

        (text completely destroyed for rest of line 6 and half of line 7 except for two insignificant patches)

§ 23   ...](-)mi-zi |INFANS-ní-zi-i x x[...

§ 24   [mi-pa-wa/i]-mi-i-tú-*a |("*314")ka-pi-la-li-na (FILIA)tú-wa/i-tara/i-na (FEMINA.PURUS.INFRA)ta-ni-ti-na |i-zi-i-wa/i-i

§ 25   wa/i-mu-´ |"AUDIRE+MI"-ti-i-tá |za-a-sa |"CAELUM-si" -i-sa|| (DEUS)TONITRUS[...]

§ 26   wa/i-mu[-*a] |DARE.CR[US?] mi-i-n[a]-*a |("*314")k[a]-pi-la-li-i-na

§ 27   wa/i-tá-*a |ARHA |CAPUT *69(-)i-ti-[x]

§ 28   pa-si-pa-[wa/i]-*a |INFANS[...

§ 29   pa-si-pa-wa/i-*a (FILIA)tú-wa/i-ta[ra/i-na] FE[MINA ...

§ 1   [I am ...], the [...] Country King, great-grandson of Hapatilas, son of the ruler Ariyahinas.

§§ 2-6	The Storm God of Heaven, King Ea, the Good God Kuparmas, the god Matilis, Teššub, the Moon God of Harran, and Kubaba loved me, the first born child.[134] They loved [...], and they granted me my paternal succession. The frontiers [..., and] the city Masuwari: I raised (its) head up to the sky. And I turned ...
§§ 7-9	And when [my great-]grandfather [was ki]ng, he was lord of his property. He ruled in the west and in the east.
§§ 10-12	But when he died in the country Ana, because his relative(?) despised my father (as) a child, he took over his succession by violence.
§§ 13-18	Afterwards his son Hamiyatas elevated it. He [...]-ed me up to my great-grandfather's succession. He made [me] lord of his own house, and he made me greater than his brothers. And everyone obeyed me.
§§ 18-20	But when he died, his son decreed evil for me, and he desired bad things for my property.
§§ 21-24	And I [raised up] my hand[s] to this Storm God of Heaven, and [to him I spoke those words:[135] "...] sons [...], and I shall make the daughter of my enemy a temple servant for him."
§§ 25-29	And he, the Storm God of Heaven, heard me, and he gave me my enemy, and I destroy[ed] (his) head. And his son[s I ...ed], and his daughter [I made] a temple serv[ant ...

2.5.2. KARABURUN

This late-eighth century B.C.E. rock inscription records a pact between two people, both called Sipis, a king Sipis and Sipis, son of Nis. The text states that the two men built a fortress together, yet the largest part of the text is given over to curses protecting both partners from one another as well as safe-guarding the inscription. The priorities here are very different from, for example, the short building inscriptions from Hama.[136]

1	§ 1	za-wa/i ha+ra/i-ni-sà-za tá-ti-zi AVUS-ha-zi ARHA ha-ta+ra/i?
	§ 2	a-wa/i si-pi-sá REX-ta
	§ 3	si-pi-sa-pa-wa/i ¹ni-ia-sa |LEPUS+ra/i-ia-la-ta
	§ 4	ha+ra/i-ni-sà-za ta-ma-ta
	§ 5	wa/i-ra+a za-ti sà-ma-za i-zi-ia-ta

---

134. For *ayala-* "first born" see Rieken and Yakubovich 2010: 212.
135. Most of the prayer is lost.
136. Cf. pp. 60–64.

	§ 6	"SCALPRUM"-*wa/i wa-mi*-LITUUS-*ta*
2	§ 7	*si-pi-sa-pa-wa/i* REX-*sa* ‖REL-*ti si-pi-ia ni-ia-sa-na* MALUS-*za* CUM-*ni za+ra/i-ti-ti-i ni-mu-wa/i-zi ni-pa-wa/i ha-ma-si*
	§ 8	*si-pi-ia-pa-wa/i-ta* REX-*ti hara/i-na-wa/i-ni-sa*(URBS) (DEUS)*ku+*AVIS-*ia ku-ma-pi ta-wa/i* PES-*zi-ha* INFRA *á-za-tu*
3	§ 9	*si-pi-sa-pa-wa/i ni-ia-sa* REL-*ti si-pi-ia* REX-*ti* MALUS-*za* CUM-*ni* ‖ *za<+ra/i>-ti-ti ni-mu-wa/i-zi ni-pa-wa/i ha-ma-si*
	§ 10	*si-pi-ia-pa-wa/i-ta ni-ia-sá-na hara/i-na-wa/i-ni-sa*(URBS) (DEUS)*ku+*AVIS-*ia ku-ma-pi ta-wa/i* INFRA-*ta á-za-tu*
	§ 11	*za-ia-pa-wa/i-ta* REL-*za-ma-ia* REL-*sa* ARHA "MALLEUS"-*ia*
	§ 12	*á-pa-ti-pa-wa/i* REX *ha+ra/i-na-wa/i-ni-sá* (DEUS) LUNA+*MI-sá ki-hara/i-ni(-)za+ra/i-ti* INFRA(-)*sá-tu*
	§ 13	SUPER+*ra/i-pa-wa/i-tu-ta ni-i ma-nu-ha pu-tu* ‖
		(above)
	§ 14	*wa/i-na-sa* SCRIBA-*la-sá*

§§ 1–6	The fathers and grandfathers demolished this fortress. And Sipis was King and Sipis, son of Nis was governor: they built the fortress. They made it together, they found ....[137]
§§ 7–10	If King Sipis desires evil for Sipis, son of Nis, for (his) son or grandson, for King Sipis may the (God) of Harran together with Kubaba swallow up (his) eyes and feet! And if Sipis, son of Nis desires evil for King Sipis, for (his) son or grandson, for Sipis son of Nis may the (God) of Harran together(?) with Kubaba swallow down (his) eyes!
§§ 11–13	Who(ever) shall erase these engravings, may the King of Harran, the Moon God, be down(?) on/for the KIHARANI (and) heart, and may he by no means PU up for him!
§ 14	Wanas (was) the scribe.

---

137. "SCALPRUM"-*wa/i*: underlying word unknown, the logogram seems to point towards an object made of stone.

2.5.3. BULGARMADEN

This rock inscription was commissioned by the ruler Tarhunazas and records how he was given a mountain, Mt. Muti, by his overlord Warpalawas, who ruled at least 738–710 B.C.E.

1 §1 *á-mu-wa/i-mi-i* |TONITRUS-*hu-na-*(LITUUS)*á-za-sá-´* |IUDEX-*ni-sa* |TONITRUS-*hu-wa/i+ra/i-**273-*sa* |(INFANS) *ni-mu-wa/i-za-sá* |*wa/i+ra/i-pa-la-wa/i-si-sa* |REX-*ti-sa* |HEROS-*ti-i-sá* |IUDEX-*ni-sa* SERVUS-*ta₄/i₄-sa*

2 §2 |*a-wa/i-ta* |*á-mi-i* |DOMINUS-*ni-i* || *wa/i+ra/i-pa-la-wa/i-ia-´* |REX-*ti-i* |("BONUS")*wa/i-sà-za-ha*

§3 *wa/i-mu-u* (DEUS)MONS-*ti-na* |*mu-ti-na* |*pi-ia-ta*

§4 |*wa/i-ma-na* (DEUS)TONITRUS-*hu-za* (DEUS)*ku*-AVIS-*pa-pa-sa-ha* |*pa+ra/i-na* ARHA |*la+ra/i-ta*

§5 |*wa/i-ta-´* |*tara/i-zi-ha*

3 §6 |*a-wa/i* REGIO-*ni* |PRAE-*i-ha* |*zí+ra/i-la-mi-i* || |("SCALPRUM.ARGENTUM")*su-ha-pa-na-ti* |*ta-ta-ha* |*á-mi-ti* |IUDEX-*na-ti* |*á-mi-ia-ti-ha-´* |*ha-tà-sà-tara/i-ma-ti*

§7 |"*MARA/I*!"-*i-sa-pa-wa/i* |(DEUS)CERVUS₂-*ti-ia-sá-ti-i* |(BONUS)*wa/i-sa₅+ra/i-ti-i* |*á-mi-i* |DOMINUS-*ni-i* ‹(BESTIA)›*HWI-sa₅+ra/i-´* |*pa*(+*ra/i?*)-*ti-i u-ta-ti-na-ha-´*

§8 |*á-mi-ha-wa/i-ta-´* |DOMINUS-*ni-na wa/i+ra/i-pa-la-wa/i-na-´*
4 |*w*[*a/i-s*]*u-u* || *u-sa-nu-sá-ha*

§9 |*á-p*[*a*]-*sa-pa-wa/i-mu-u* |("ASINUS")*tara/i-ka-sa-ni-ia-za* (*92) *za-la-la* |("ARGENTUM.DARE")*pi-ia-ta-´*

§10 |*HWI-sa-pa-wa/i-ti-i mu-ti-ia* (DEUS)MONS-*ti* |*ha-*‹*zi*›-*ia-ni-sá-´* |‹*i-zi*›-*ia-ti-i*

§11 *a-wa/i* |TONITRUS-*hu-na-*(LITUUS)*á-za-sa-za-´* DEUS-*na-za* |"OVIS"-*ru-pi* |*sa₅-sa₅+ra/i-la-i* |"ANNUS"-*na* ANNUS-*na*||

5 §12 *wa/i-ru-ta* |*mu-ti-ia-wa/i-ni-zi* DEUS-*ni-zi* |*wa/i-su-u* |PES-*wa/i-i‹-tu?›*

§13 |*za-pa-wa/i-ta-´* |"CAPERE"-*ma-z*[*a*] *HWI-sa* |ARHA-´ |*ha+ra/i-ri+i*

§14 |*á-pa-*‹*x*› CAPUT-*ti-na* (DEUS)TONITRUS-*z*[*a?*] DEUS-*ni-zi-ha* |ARHA |"DELERE"-*nú-tu*

§ 15 |(DEUS)LUNA+*MI-pa-wa/i-na* |*ha+ra/i-tu*
§ 16   (DEUS)*ni-ka-ru-ha-sa-pa-wa/i-na* AR[*HA*] EDERE-*t*[*u*]
§ 17   (DEUS)*ku-pa-wa/i-na* "XX"-*tu-i*

§§ 1–4   I (am) the ruler Tarhunazas, son of Tarhuwara-*273, servant of King Warpalawas, Hero, Ruler. I was good to my lord, King Warpalawas, and he gave to me the divine Mt. Muti.[138] And the Storm God and Kubaba prospered it for me.

§§ 5–9   I turned it, and because of my justice and my wisdom, I stood out[139] in the land ZIRALAMI SUHAPANATI. Through the goodness of Runtiyas of the Countryside, I UTATINA-ed[140] wild beasts there(?) for my lord. I was very good to my lord Warpalawas, and he sold me wagons for the mules.

§§ 10–12   Who(ever) shall make himself governor for the divine Mt. Muti, he shall offer to Tarhunazas's gods sacrificial sheep[141] every year. And the Gods of Muti shall come well for him.

§§ 13–17   But who(ever) shall smash this record, may the Storm God and the gods destroy that person, may the Moon God smash him, may Nikaruhas eat him up, may Kubaba ... him!

2.5.4. ASSUR Letters

Handwritten Luwian texts are very few in number, the main representative of this group are six letters of a merchant to his suppliers written on lead strips.[142] These were discovered in 1905 during excavations at Assur, and we assume that they came to this city as booty in antiquity. They were found rolled up, buried under the floor of a house together with an Old-Assyrian cuneiform tablet, possibly because they were thought to hold magical properties. The letters may have been executed in the vicinity of Karkamiš and date to the eighth century B.C.E.

These letters record the correspondence between various merchants, and concern the supply of goods. Both sender and addressee vary, which makes one

---

138. Mountains were generally thought of as divine; this is also indicated by the writing system: one of the two hieroglyphic symbols for mountain shows a mountain deity, sign *4 = *207b, while the other, sign *207a, shows the contours of a mountain surrounded by the glyph for the divine.

139. For PRAE-*I tata-* "to stand out," see Rieken 2004: 467 quoting Melchert.

140. Hapax legomenon.

141. (OVIS)*kurupi-* seems to denote a specific sacrificial sheep whereas (OVIS)*hawi-* refers to sheep in general.

142. For an examination of the handwriting see Payne, 2005.

wonder why these letters were kept together. Maybe they were copies kept by the scribe who wrote them? Or should one imagine a group of merchants working together and therefore keeping their correspondence together, too? As these letters lack comparative texts, they contain a higher number of words unknown to us.

ASSUR letter a

1   § 1 |á-sa$_5$-za |REL-pa-ti-wa/i+ra/i-ia |ta-ka-sa-la-sa-wa/i^{-i} |("LOQUI)ha-ri+i-ti-i

     § 2 |sa-na-wa/i+ra/i |PUGNUS.PUGNUS-si

     § 3 |a-za$_5$-za-ha-wa/i-za |á-pi |ha-tu-ra+a

2   § 4 |u-nu-ha-wa/i-tu-u-ta |u-za-ri+i ARHA-´ || pa+ra/i-ra+a-ha

     § 5 |wa/i-mu^{-i} |ha-tu+ra/i-na |NEG$_2$-´ |ma-nu-ha |("LOQUI"$^{(-´)}$)pu-pa-la-ta

     § 6 |NEG$_2$-a-wa/i |tara/i-pa^{-i}-mi-i-sa |za-na |a-pa-ha ("PES$_2$") a+ra/i-ta-´ |ka+ra/i-mi-sà(URBS)

3   § 7   (*205)á-tu-ni-na-wa/i-mu |REL-za |NEG$_2$-´ |ma-nu-ha || |VIA-wa/i-ni-ta

     § 8 |ARHA-ha-wa/i-mu-u |REL-ri̯+i MORI-ha-na

     § 9 |wa/i-mu-u |u-za+ra/i^{-i} |("*476.*311")a-li-ia-ta

     § 10 |u-nu-ha-wa/i-mu-u (BESTIA)HWI-sá-na-ma-ia |ha-la+ra/i-la

4 |*472(-)ma^{-i}-sa$_5$+ra/i-zi^{-i} 3-zi-i |ni-pa-wa/i || 4-zi |("*78")a-ru-ti-zi |("LEPUS")ta-pa-sà-la-ia-´ |("*286.*317")wa/i-ara/i-ma |VIA-wa/i-ni^{-i}

     § 11 |("FEMINA(?)")sà-nu-ta-sa-ha-wa/i-mu |(*187)zú-mi-la-zi-i 50 VIA-wa/i-ni

     § 12 |ha-ti-ia-pa-wa/i-mu |("*286.*317")wa/i+ra/i-ma-´ |za-ia |VIA-wa/i-ni

ASSUR letter b

1   § 1 |á-sa$_5$-za |DOMUS-ni-wa/i+ra/i-ia |ta-ka-sa-la-sa-wa/i-´ <LOQUI ... ?>

     § 2 |sa-na-wa/i+ra/i^{-i} |PUGNUS.PUGNUS-si

§ 3 |á-mu-ha-wa/i-mu |á-pi |ha-tu-ra+a

§ 4 |u-nu-^{i}-pa-wa/i-mu |1-ti-na |za-na |("LOQUI")ma-ra+a-ti-na |CUM-ni |i-zi-ia-´

§ 5 |a-wa/i || |á-pi |ku-ru-pi |REL-ia |("*286.*317")$^{(-´)}$wa/i-ra+a-ma |LEPUS-pa-sà-la-ia |ARHA-´ |("*69")sa-ha-na

§ 6 |wa/i-ra+a |("*69")ha+ra/i-za

§ 7 |wa/i-ma-ra+a |ARHA-^{i} |VIA-wa/i-ni

§ 8 |("CANIS")zú-wa/i-ni-zi-ha-wa/i |a-pa-zi |REL-ri+i-´ |a-sa-ti

§ 9 |a-wa/i |2-zi-i || |sa-na-wa/i-i-zi ("*481")wa/i+ra/i-mu-ta-li-zi |PUGNUS-ri+i-´

§ 10 wa/i-mu-u |VIA-wa/i-ni

ASSUR letter c

§ 1 |á-sa$_5$-za-wa/i |ka-ka-ia |REL-si-si-ti-mi-ha |ta-ka-sa-la-sa-wa/i ("LOQUI"-´)ha-ri+i-ti

§ 2 |á-pi-wa/i-za |ha-tu-ra+a

§ 3 |á-ta$_5$/i$_5$-mí-sa-sa-ha-wa/i+ra/i

§ 4 |u-za$_5$-za||-wa/i-ma-za |ha-tu-ra+a

§ 5 |á-pi-ha-wa/i-tu-u-ta |ni-i-´ ARHA-´ |ma-nu-ha pa+ra/i-ra+a-wa/i

§ 6 |á-pi-ha-wa/i-mu-ta |NEG$_2$-´ |REL-ha-na |u-si-ti-sa

§ 7 |wa/i-mu-ta |*187(-)tu-wa/i-i-za |REL-za |u-si-ti-sà ||

§ 8 |wa/i-mu-u |10 ha-sà-pi-na |100-ha-wa/i-mu "(*187)zú"-mi-la-a-na |VIA-wa/i-ni

§ 9 ("LEPUS.ANIMAL")ta-pa-sà-la-ia-ha-wa/i |(*286.*317)wa/i-ra+a-ma^i |REL-ta-ha LITUUS+na-ti-sà 4-zi || |ni-pa-wa/i |5-na-´ |("*78")a-ru-ti-na

§ 10 wa/i-mu-u |VIA-wa/i-ni

§ 11 |ha-la+ra/i-la-ha-wa/i-mu-u |sa-na-wa/i-ia |VIA-wa/i-ni

ASSUR letter d

1 § 1 |á-sa$_5$-za-wa/i |[DOM]US-ni-*375-[…]-ia^{-i} [|ta]-ka-sa^{-i}-[la-s]á-wa/i [|("LOQ]UI")ha-ri+i-ti-´

§ 2 |sa-na-wa/i+ra/i |PUGNUS.PUGNUS-si

§ 3 |sa-pi-su+ra/i-ha-wa/i-ri+i

§ 4 |á-za$_5$-za-ha^{-i}-wa/i-za |á-pi ha-tu-ra+a ||

2 § 5 |wa/i-za |NEG$_2$-´ |REL-ha-na |ha-tu+ra/i-na^{-i} |ha-tu-ra+a^{-i}

§ 6 |u-nu-pa-wa/i-mu-u |sa-na-wa/i^{-i}-i-zi^{-i} |("*91")á-tu-ti-zi |(VIA)ha+ra/i-wa/i-ni

§ 7 |*472(-)ma-sa$_5$+ra/i-zi-ha-wa/i-mu$^!$ |(VIA)ha+ra/i-wa/i-ni

3 § 8 |"SCUTUM"(-)ha+ra/i-ti-ha-wa/i-mu || |hara/i-li-na |sa-na-wa/i- zi-na^{-i} |VIA-wa/i-ni

§ 9 |DOMINUS-ni-wa/i |(*91)za-la-la-si-na |REL-ti-sà-mi-na^{-i} |(VIA)ha+ra/i-wa/i-ni

§ 10 |ni-wa/i-mu^{-i} |á-pi |NEG$_2$-´ |VIA-wa/i-ni-si |

ASSUR letter e

1 § 1 |á-sa$_5$-za [|]pi-ha-mi |hara/i-na-wa/i-za-sa-wa/i ("LOQUI"-´) ha-ri+i-ti

§ 2 [|]sa-pi-su+ra/i-wa/i-a-ti

§ 3 |u-sa-ta-mu-ti-sà-ha-wa/i-´ |ha-tu+ra/i-´

§ 4 |a-za$_5$-za-ha-wa/i-za |á-pi |ha-tu-ra+a

§ 5 |wa/i-za |NEG$_2$-´ |REL-i-ha |ha-tu+ra/i-na |ha-tu-ra+a

§ 6 |wa/i-ma-za |u-za$_5$-za |ha-tu-ra+a |a-sa-ta-ni

§ 7 |a-wa/i |á-pi |u-zi-na |REL-i |ha-tu+ra/i-na |AUDIRE+MI-ta-ra+a-nu

§ 8 |wa/i-za |á-pi |a-za$_5$-za-ha |ha-tu+ra/i-´ ||

2 § 9 ni-pa-wa/i-na |á-mu |REL-za |i-zi-ia-wa/i |á-mi-na |za-na |ha-tu+ra/i-na

§ 10 |(COR)na-hu-ti-zi-wa/i-mu |za-zi |INFANS-ni-zi |REL-i |("*460")á-sa-ta-ri+i |("COR")ta-wa/i-sà-ta-ti-ha |su-ti-ri+i-ti |ha+ra/i-ta-ti-ha |PRAE-na |ARHA-´ |(MORI)wa/i-wa/i-ri+i-ta-ti

§ 11 |REL-i-sà-wa/i-sa |á-mi-sa |ha-tu-<ra+>a-sa

§ 12 |u-nu-ha-wa/i-ma-za-ta |ní-i |ma-nu-ha |ARHA-´ ("COR") pa+ra/i-ra+a-ia |DOMINUS-ni-i |a-za-ia-ha-´ |sa-na-wa/i-ia

§ 13 |wa/i-za^{-i} |ni-i |ARHA |("*69")sa-tu^{-i}

§ 14 |ni-pa-wa/i-mu || ARHA-´ |MORI-nu^{-i}

§ 15 |á-ta$_5$/i$_5$-wa/i-za |REL-sà-ha |a-sa-ti

§ 16 |NEG$_2$-wa/i-ma-za-´[|?]u-za$_5$-za

§ 17 |á-ta$_5$/i$_5$-ha-wa/i-ma-za |u-za$_5$-za

§ 18 |*179.*347.5(-)wa/i-sà-pa-ha-wa/i-mu |FEMINA-ti-na^{-i} |VIA-wa/i-ni^{-i}

§ 19 |zi-pa-wa/i-na |("*69")sa-na-tu

§ 20 |wa/i-na-´ |*187(-)wa/i-ia-ni-tu

§ 21 |DOMINUS-ni-ha-wa/i *179.*347.5 |sa-na-wa/i |a-ta^{-i} |PUG-NUS-ri+i^{-i}

§ 22 |a-wa/i |OMNIS-MI-za |CUM-ni |PONERE-u

§ 23 |a-ta-ha-wa/i-´ |*179(-)REL-la-ia-na-na |sa-na-wa/i-zi-na-´ |*179(-)sà-la/i/u-ma-sa-ha-wa/i |VIA-wa/i-ni

§ 24 a-wa/i |FLUMEN.DOMINUS-ia || ("PES$_2$")pa-tu

§ 25 |a-wa/i-wa/i-mu-ta |"*198"(-)ki+ra/i-ra+a-za |*317.CRUS$_2$-pa-sa-za-ha |SUPER+ra/i-ha |"LONGUS"(-)ia-ti-na-ia

§ 26 |*308-mi-sa-ha-wa/i-mu^{-i} *351.*406-ia-sa$_5$+ra/i-za

§ 27 |zú+ra/i-wa/i-za-ha^{-i}-wa/i-mu-u |*317-ni-za |VIA-wa/i-ni

§ 28 |hi-pa+ra/i-wa/i-ni-ha-wa/i-za |INFANS-ni-na VIA-wa/i-ni^{-i}

§ 29 |*198(-)ki+ra/i-ti-zi-wa/i |*317.CRUS$_2$-pa-sa-ha REL-i-sà (LITUUS)u-ni-ti

§ 30 |INFANS-ni-ha-wa/i-mu |tu-wa/i-na CUM-ni *77-ti-sa

§ 31 |PRAE-wa/i |á-mu |na-wa/i-´ |REL-na |REL-sà-ha-´ (LITUUS)u-ni-ti

ASSUR letter f+g

f1 § 1 |*á-sa₅-za* |*i-ia-mi* |*ma-mu-ti-ha* |*ta-ka-sa-la-sa-wa*/i⁻ⁱ |*ma-mu-sa-ha* |("LOQUI")*ha-ti-i-ti*

§ 2 |*sa-pi-su+ra*/*i-´-wa*/*i-ma-za*

§ 3 |*a-za₅-a-za-ha-wa*/*i-za* |*á-pi* |*ha-tu-ra+a*

§ 4 |*a-wa*/*i* |"COR"(-)*na-hi-zi* "COR"(-)*la+ra*/*i-hi-ri+i-ia-zi-ha* |PRAE-*i* |(PONERE)*sà-ti-nu⁻ⁱ*

§ 5 |*wa*/*i-za-´* |*na-a-pa* |*a-su-nu*

§ 6 |"*474"(-)*hi-sà-wa*/*i* |(BRACCHIUM)*hu-mi+ra*/*i-ha* |*zi-ku-na-ti* |ARHA |*wa*/*i-la-mi-na-´* |PUGNUS.PUGNUS-*nu*

§ 7 |"*476"-*wa*/*i-pa-wa*/*i* ("*476.*311")*hi-ru-ra+a-ti⁻ⁱ* |ARHA |*wa*/*i-la-u-ta* ||

f2 § 8 |*su-ti-ri+i-na-wa*/*i-´* |*ha+ra*/*i-ta-ha* |PRAE-*i* (PONERE)*sà-ti-nu⁻ⁱ*

§ 9 |REL-*sà-´-wa*/*i-sa-´* |*a-zi-sa* |*ha-tu-ra+a-sa*

§ 10 |*u-nu-pa-wa*/*i-za* |NEG₂-*´* |*tu-wa*/*i-ri+i* |*ha-tu-ra+a*

§ 11 |*wa*/*i-ri+i⁻ⁱ* |*ku-ma-na* |*ha-tu-ra+a*

§ 12 |*wa*/*i-za* |*ni-i-´* |*ma-nu-ha* |ARHA-*´* |("*69")*sa-si⁻ⁱ*

§ 13 *ni-pa-wa*/*i-mu* |("SIGILLUM")HWI-*pa-sa-nu*

§ 14 |*á-ta₅*/*i₅-wa*/*i-za* |REL-*sà-ha* |*a-sa-ti*

§ 15 |*wa*/*i-tu-u-ta* |*ni-i-´* |*ma-nu-ha* |"*356"(-)‹REL-*zú*›[…] |2 […] |[…]-*z*[*a*/*i*…]||

f3 § 16 [|*á*]-*pi*-[*ha-wa*/i]-*´* [|…]-*la*-[…](URBS) [|]*á-pa-ti* |INFANS-*ni-i* |*ha+ra*/*i-na-i-na* |CUM-*ni-´* |*77-*ha-´* |*tu-u* |VERSUS-*na*

§ 17 |*wa*/*i-na* |*ni-i* |REL-*sà-ha* LITUUS+*na-ri+i-´*

§ 18 |*pa+ra*/*i-la-ri+i-*|ꜝ*ha-wa*/*i-tu-u* |("*205")*á-tu-na-ri+i* |REL-*na-´* |("*69")*wa*/*i-za-na* |("*69")*wa*/*i-zi-ha-na*

§ 19 |*wa*/*i-za* |OMNIS-*MI-za* |"VIA"-*wa*/*i-ni*

§ 20 |*á-pi-wa*/*i-za-´* |NEG₂-*´* |REL-*ha-na* |*a-sa-ti*

§ 21 |*á-pi-ha-wa*/*i-za* |ASINUS.ANIMAL-*na-zi* |*a-pa-zi* |ARHA-*´* |MORI-*ta* ||

	§ 22	|u-nu-pa-wa/i-tu-u |(ASINUS₂.ANIMAL)tara/i-ka-sa-ni-sa |REL-ri+i |a-sa-ti
f4	§ 23	wa/i-mu-u |VIA-wa/i-ni
	§ 24	|a-wa/i-wa/i |("PES")pa+ra/i-ri+i |ARHA-´ |("PES₂")a+ra/i-wa/i
	§ 25	|wa/i-ma-na |(VIA)ha+ra/i-wa/i-ni
	§ 26	|á-pi-wa/i-ma-na |ni-i-´ |NEG₂-´ |VIA-wa/i-ni-si
	§ 27	|á-pi-ha-wa/i-za |(*420)wa/i-sa-ha-sa |REL-za |VIA-wa/i-ni-ta
	§ 28	|wa/i-za |á-pi 4-zi⁻ⁱ |ka-mara/i-zi |i-sa-u-ta
	§ 29	|wa/i-za-ta |"COR"-ta-ni |POST-na-´ *480-ia
g"3"	§ 30	|PRAE-pa-wa/i-za-ta || |NEG₂-´ |REL-sà-ha |"PES₂"(-)wa/i-´-za-sa-ti
	§ 31	|wa/i-za |ka-mara/i-ra+a-na |REL-i-ha |VIA-wa/i-ni⁻ⁱ
	§ 32	|ni-pa-wa/i-tu-u-´ |NEG₂-´ ‹|a›-sa-ti
	§ 33	‹|a›-wa/i ‹|á›-pi [|DOMUS]-ni-wa/i+ra/i-ia [|(X)]á-mu+ra/i[-?]-la/i/u+ra/i-´‹|a›-sa-ti
	§ 34	‹|wa/i›-tu-u-wa/i-na ‹|CUM›-ni-´ |i-ia-sa
	§ 35	|wa/i-za-na |VIA-wa/i-ni-i
	§ 36	|a-la-wa/i-ra+a-ti-ha-wa/i-mu(URBS) |("CORNU")zú+ra/i-ni || BIBERE-u-na-sa |sa-na-wa/i-ia |MAGNUS+ra/i-ia-´ |VIA-wa/i-ni⁻ⁱ
g"4"	§ 37	|á-pi-ha-wa/i-´ |("LEPUS")ta-pa-sà-la-ia |("*286.*317")wa/i-ara/i-ma-´ |ku-ru-pi |á-mi-i |a-ta-ti |ARHA-´("*69")sa-ha-na
	§ 38	|á-pa⁻ⁱ-ia-pa-wa/i |DOMUS-ni-i |a-ta-ti ARHA-´ |("*69")sa-ha-´
	§ 39	|wa/i-ra+a⁻ⁱ |("*69")ha+ra/i-za
	§ 40	|wa/i-ma-ra+a ARHA-´ |VIA-wa/i-ni ||
g"1"	§ 41	|á-pi-wa/i-ra+a⁻ⁱ |11 ("*78")a-ru-ti-sá
	§ 42	|ni-pa-wa/i+ra/i⁻ⁱ |NEG₂-´ |wa/i-mi-LITUUS-si
	§ 43	|a-wa/i⁻ⁱ |LITUUS+na-ti-sa |REL-ta-ha |10 ("*78")a-ru-ti-na
	§ 44	|wa/i-mu-u |VIA-wa/i-ni⁻ⁱ
	§ 45	|á-pi-ha-wa/i+ra/i-ta |hara/i-na-wa/i+ra/i-sa |("PANIS.SCU-TELLA")tu-ni-ka-ra+a-sa |ARHA-´ |OCCIDENS(-)la/i/u-si-ta

TEXTS

§ 46 |wa/i-na-´ |("*69")ha+ra/i-za

g"2" § 47 |wa/i-za-na ARHA-´ || |VIA-wa/i-ni^{-i}

§ 48 |a-wa/i-wa/i-za |PANIS-ni-na^{-i} |NEG$_2$-´ |a-sa-ti

§ 49 |REL-sà-wa/i-z[a] |pi-i[a...] |ha+ra/i-n[a?-...]

§ 50 |á-[...]-za-[...] (LITUUS)ti-[ia]-ri+i-[...]

§ 51 |wa/i-[ri+i]-ia-sa-ta |ni-i^{-i} |ARHA^{-i} |OCCIDENS(-)la/i/u^{-i}-si-ti-i

§ 52 |ti-ha-wa/i-za |tu-wa/i-na |INFANS-ni-na CUM-ni *77-ti-sa

§ 53   wa/i-za LITUUS+na-ri+i

ASSUR letter a:

§§ 1–4   Say to Kwipatiwaris, Taksalas speaks: ⌜"(May) you live well! Must we write back? Now I missed you by your (letter).

§§ 5–9   Did not Tarpamis come now and then to Karkamiš? Why did he by no means send the ATUNI? (For) me (it is) as (if) we had died. You ALIYAed me with your (letter).

§§ 10–12   Now, send me wild animals(?), HALARALA,[143] MASARIs[144] 3 or 4 baskets, urgent(?) orders(?)! And send me 50 ZUMILA[145] of SANUTA. Send me these original orders(?)!"

ASSUR letter b:

§§ 1–2   Say to Parniwaris, Taksalas <speaks>: "(May) you live well! Must I write back?

§§ 3–7   But now do this first request for me: the sacrificial sheep, which we left behind, urgent(?) orders(?), collect[146] them, and send them out to me!

§§ 8–10   And if those dogs are (there), pick two good WARMUTALIs, and send (them) to me!"

---

143. Recurs letter c § 11.
144. Recurs letter d § 7.
145. Recurs letter c § 8.
146. See Melchert 1988: 220–24.

ASSUR letter c:

§§ 1-4   Say to Kakas and Kwisisitimis, Taksalas speaks: "Must we write back? You are arrogant![147] You must write!
§§ 5-7   Further, let me by no means miss you, and further, you bring me nothing! Why do you bring me TUWI(N)ZA?
§§ 8-11 Send me 10 HASPI and 100 ZUMILA, and urgent demands, wherever you see 4 or 5 baskets, send (them) to me, and send me good HALARALA!"

ASSUR letter d:

§§ 1-5   Say to Parni-...[...], Taksalas speaks: "(May) you live well, and peace to you! Must we write back? We must write no letter!
§§ 6-8   Now, send me good ATUTIs,[148] and send me MASARIs,[149] and send me a HARATI-shield, a good shield!
§§ 9-10 Send an approved lord of the chariot! Do not fail to send (them) back to me!"

ASSUR letter e:

§§ 1-9   Say to Pihamis, Haranawizas speaks: "Peace with you! You are falling in error(?) as regards writing! Must we write back ourselves? We must write no letter, you must write! Hear your kind of letter back! Do we need to write back? Or why did I make it, this letter of mine?
§§ 10-17 Because these worrisome(?) children are dying before(?) me from (evil) spells,[150] SUTIRI of the eyes and HARATA.[151] What (is) it, my letter? And now let our lord's and our goods miss you in no way, and may they not let us go, nor cause me to die! Whoever (is) right(?)[152] to us, you yourselves are not, you (are) right(?) for yourselves!
§§ 18-24 Send me a woman (for?) WASAPA! Here let them SAN her, and let them WIYANI her! For the lord, raise WASAPA well, put all

---

147. See Rieken and Yakubovich 2010: 212.
148. The determinative *91 tells us that this word must belong to the realm of chariots.
149. As this letter seems to be concerned with goods relating to chariots and warfare, I would expect MASARI to belong to either sphere.
150. Cf. Melchert (1993: 37), s.u. *asta-*.
151. SUTIRI and HARATA recur in letter f+g § 8.
152. See Rieken and Yakubovich 2010: 214; also letter f § 14.

together, and therein send good KWALAYANA and SALAMASA, and let it/them go to the river-lord.

§§ 25–31 ...[153] And send me ZUR(A)WA/I(N)ZA *317-NI(N)ZA,[154] and send us the child Hiparawanis, who knows KIRATIs and ... PASA.[155] You pledge(?)[156] your child to me, whom no one shall know before me!"[157]

ASSUR letter f+g:

§§ 1–3 Say to Iyamis and company, Taksalas and company speak: "Peace to you! Must we write back?

§§ 4–8 Cause to put(?) forth NAHIs and LARAHIRIYAs, cause us good NAPA, cause the eunuchs(?) and the HUMIRA, dead from ZIKUNA, to live! ... they died from the oath. Cause to put(?) forth SUTIRI and HARATA.[158]

§§ 9–13 Since you must write, by no means abandon us, nor cause me harm!

§§ 14–17 Who(ever) is right(?)[159] to us, let [...] by no means KWISU[...] to you 2 [...]. Further [in?] the city [Al]la[wara][160] in your presence I pledged HARNAIS for that child. Let no one see her![161]

§§ 18–20 With PARLA ATUNI, the demand which we demanded of you, send (it) all to us! There remains nothing to us.

§§ 21–26 Further, those donkeys have died on us. Now, if you have a mule, send (it) to us! Come, shall I walk out (and about) on foot? Send it to me, do not fail to send it back to me![162]

---

153. Not much sense can be made of §§ 25–26.

154. On luw. *sura-, zura-* see most recently Simon forthcoming.

155. The unknown *198(-)kirati and *317.CRUS$_2$-*pasa-* were already mentioned in § 25.

156. The verb is written logographically with *77, possibly showing a hand placed into another hand.

157. This seems to refer to a marriage arrangement. It is therefore likely that the verb "know' is used in the biblical sense.

158. Cf. letter e § 10.

159. See Rieken and Yakubovich 2010: 214.

160. Restoration based on city name occurring in § 36.

161. We might also understand this sentence as a ban of sexual relationship before marriage.

162. I.e., send me what I demanded, do not send another letter back refusing or discussing this issue. The two "it"s do not refer to the same thing.

§§ 27-35 Further, what did they send us of the purchase(?)? They bought for us another four KAMARA. After us one may *480[163] their person, but before us no one may carry them off. Send us some KAMARA, or (if) you do not have any, and AMURALURA remains to [Par]niwaris: buy it from him and send it to us!"

§§ 36-40 From the city Alawara send me good, big drinking-horns! Further urgent orders: we left behind sacrificial sheep in my rooms(?).[164] I left those behind in the house, in the room: lay hold of them and send them out to me!

§§ 41-47 Further, they (are) 11 baskets, or (if) you do not find them, wherever you see 10 baskets, send (them) to me! Further, the baker Haranawaris has gone west(?) (i.e., disappeared). Lay hold of him, and send him over to us!

§§ 48-53 Come, there is no bread to us, who will give us HARNA[...]? Watch t[hat man] for us, let him not go west(?)! You pledge your child to us, and she will see us."

---

163. The logogram is unknown; it looks like a dagger. Sense: "harm, injure"?

164. *anta* "inside," thus *a(n)tati-* "inside space, room" in analogy with Lycian *ñte* "inside," *ñtata-* "burial chamber."

Text Publications

ALEPPO 2: Hawkins 2000, 235–38.
ASSUR letters: Hawkins 2000, 533–55.
BABYLON 1: Hawkins 2000, 391–94.
BABYLON 2: Hawkins 2000, 394–97.
BABYLON 3: Hawkins 2000, 394–97.
BOHÇA: Hawkins 2000, 478–80.
BULGARMADEN: Hawkins 2000, 521–25.
CEKKE: Hawkins 2000, 143–51.
ÇİNEKÖY: Tekoğlu and Lemaire 2000, 961–1007.
HAMA 1–3, 6–7: Hawkins 2000, 411–14.
HINES: Hawkins 2000, 407–9.
KARABURUN: Hawkins 2000, 480–83.
KARKAMIŠ A1b: Hawkins 2000, 91–92.
KARKAMIŠ A2+3: Hawkins 2000, 108–12.
KARKAMIŠ A4d: Hawkins 2000, 100–101.
KARKAMIŠ A5b: Hawkins 2000, 185–86.
KARKAMIŠ A6: Hawkins 2000, 123–28.
KARKAMIŠ A15b: Hawkins 2000, 130–33.
KARKAMIŠ A11a: Hawkins 2000, 94–100.
KARKAMIŠ A11b+c : Hawkins 2000, 101–8.
KARATEPE 1: Hawkins 2000, 45–68.
KULULU 1: Hawkins 2000, 442–44.
KULULU 4: Hawkins 2000, 445–47.
MARAŞ 1: Hawkins 2000, 261–65.
MEHARDE: Hawkins 2000, 416–19.
QAL'AT EL MUDIQ: Hawkins 2000, 407–9.
RESTAN: Hawkins 2000, 407–9.
SHEIZAR: Hawkins 2000, 416–19.
SULTANHAN: Hawkins 2000, 463–72.
TALL ŠṬĪB: Gonnet 2010, 97–99.
TELL AHMAR 1: Hawkins 2000, 239–43.
TELL AHMAR 6: Hawkins 2006, 11–32.
TİLSEVET: Hawkins 2000, 178–80.
TOPADA: Hawkins 2000, 451–61.

BIBLIOGRAPHY

Bryce, T.
    1998   *The Kingdom of the Hittites*. Oxford: Oxford University Press.
    2003   "History." Pages 27–127 in *The Luwians*. Edited by H. C. Melchert. HdO 68. Leiden: Brill.
    2004   *Life and Society in the Hittite World*. Oxford: Oxford University Press.

Çambel, H.
    1999   *Corpus of Hieroglyphic Luwian Inscriptions,* Vol II: *Karatepe-Arslantaş. The Inscriptions: Facsimile Edition*. With a contribution by Wolfgang Röllig and tables by John David Hawkins. Berlin: de Gruyter.

Collins, B. J.
    2007   "The Bible, the Hittites, and the Construction of the 'Other'." Pages 153–61 in *Tabularia Hethaeorum: Hethitologische Beiträge. Silvin Kosak zum 65. Geburtstag*. Edited by D. Groddek and M. Zorman. DBH 25. Wiesbaden: Harrassowitz.

Durnford, S.
    2010   "How Old Was the Ankara Silver Bowl When Its Inscriptions Were Added?" *AnSt* 60: 51–70.

Friedrich, J., et al.
    1969   *Altkleinasiatische Sprachen*. HdO 2. Leiden: Brill.

Gerhards, M.
    2009   "Die biblischen 'Hethiter'." *WO* 39: 145–79.

Giusfredi, F.
    2010   *Sources for a Socio-Economic History of the Neo-Hittite States*. THeth 28. Heidelberg: Winter.

Goedegebuure, P.
    2007   "The Hieroglyphic Luwian demonstrative ablative-instrumentals zin and apin." Pages 319–34 in *VI. Congresso Internazionale di Ittitologia, Roma, 5–9 settembre 2005*. Edited by A. Archi and R. Francia. SMEA 49, Rome: Rivista dell'Istituto per gli Studi Micenei ed Egeo - Anatolici del CNR.

Gonnet, H.
    2010   "Une stèle hiéroglyphique louvite à Tall Štīb." Pages 97–99 in *Entre nomades et sédentaires: prospections en Syrie du Nord et en Jordanie du Sud*. Edited by P.-L. Gatier, B. Geyer, and M.-O. Rousset. TMO 55. Lyon: Maison de l'Orient et de la Méditerranée.

Hawkins, J. D.
2000 *Corpus of Hieroglyphic Luwian Inscriptions*, Vol. I: *Inscriptions of the Iron Age*. 3 vols. Berlin: de Gruyter.
2003 "Script and Texts." Pages 128–69 in *The Luwians*. Edited by H. C. Melchert. HdO 68. Leiden: Brill.
2004 "The Stag-God of the Countryside and Related Problems." Pages 355–69 in J. H. W. Penney, *Indo-European Perspectives, Studies in Honour of Anna Morpurgo Davies*. Oxford: Oxford University Press.
2006 "The Inscription." Pages 11–32 in *A New Luwian Stele and the Cult of the Storm-God at Til Barsib-Masuwari*. Tell Ahmar II. Edited by G. Bunnens. Louvain: Peeters.
2011 "The Inscriptions of the Aleppo Temple." *AnSt* 61: 35–54.

Herbordt, S.
2005 *Die Prinzen- und Beamtensiegel der hethitischen Großreichszeit auf Tonbullen aus dem Nisantepe-Archiv in Hattusa*. Boğazköy-Hattusa 19. Mainz: von Zabern.

van den Hout, Th.
2006 "Institutions, Vernaculars, Publics: the Case of Second-Millennium Anatolia." Pages 217–56 in *Margins of Writing, Origins of Cultures*. Edited by S. Sanders. Chicago: The Oriental Institute of the University of Chicago.

Houwink ten Cate, P. H. J.
1961 *The Luwian Population Groups of Lycia and Cilicia Aspera during the Hellenistic Period*. Leiden: Brill.

Hutter, M.
2003 "Aspects of Luwian Religion." Pages 211–80 in *The Luwians*. Edited by H. C. Melchert. HdO 68. Leiden: Brill.

Klengel, H.
1999 *Geschichte des hethitischen Reiches*. HdO 34. Leiden: Brill.

Laroche, E.
1960 *Les hiéroglyphes hittites, Première partie, L'écriture*. Paris: CNRS.

Marazzi, M.
1990 *Il Geroglifico Anatolico, Problemi di Analisi e Prospettive di Ricerca*. Rome: Herder.
1994 "Ma gli Hittiti scriveveano veramente su 'legno'?" Pages 131–60 in *Miscellanea di studi linguistici in onore di Walter Belardi*. P. Cipriano, P. Di Giovine, M. Mancini. Rome: Il Calamo.
1998 [2000] *Il Geroglifico Anatolico, Sviluppi della ricerca a venti anni dalla sua "ridecifrazione."* Naples: Herder.
2007 "Sigilli, sigillature e tavolette di legno: alcune considerazioni alla luce di nuovi dati." Pages 465–74 in *Belkıs Dinçol ve Ali Dinçol'a Armağan. VITA. Festschrift in Honor of Belkıs Dinçol and Ali Dinçol*. Edited by M. Alparslan, M. Doğan-Alparslan and H. Peker. İstanbul: Ege.

Melchert, H. C.
1978 "PIE velars in Luvian." Pages 182–204 in *Studies in Memory of Warren Cowgill (1929–1985)*. Edited by Calvert Watkins. Berlin/New York: De Gruyter.

1988a   "Luvian Lexical Notes." *HS* 101: 211–43
1988b   "'Thorn' and 'Minus' in Hieroglyphic Luvian Orthography." *AnSt* 38: 29–42.
1993   *Cuneiform Luvian Lexicon*. Chapel Hill, NC.
2003a   "Language." Pages 170–210 in *The Luwians*. Edited by H. C. Melchert. HdO 68. Leiden: Brill.
2003b   "Prehistory." Pages 8–26 in *The Luwians*. Edited by H. C. Melchert. HdO 68. Leiden: Brill.
2004a   *A Dictionary of the Lycian Language*. Ann Arbor: Beach Stave Press.
2004b   "A Luwian Dedication." Pages 370–79 in *Indo-European Perspectives, Studies in Honour of Anna Morpurgo Davies*. Edited by J. H. W. Penney. Oxford: Oxford University Press.
2010   "Remarks on the Kuttamuwa Inscription." *Kubaba* 1: 4–11.

Mora, C.
1995   "I Luvi e la scrittura geroglifica anatolica." Pages 275–81 in *Atti del II Congresso Internazionale di Hittitologia, Pavia, 28 giugno–2 lulio 1993*. Edited by O. Carruba, M. Giorgieri, and C. Mora. Pavia: Iuculano.

Neumann, G.
1992   *System und Ausbau der hethitischen Hieroglyphenschrift*. Nachrichten der Akademie der Wissenschaften zu Göttingen, I. Philologisch-historische Klasse, Nr. 4. Göttingen: Vandenhoeck & Ruprecht.

Payne, A.
2005   "Überlegungen zur Hieroglyphenschrift der Assur-Briefe." *MDOG* 137: 109–18.
2006   "Multilingual inscriptions and their Audiences: Cilicia and Lycia." Pages 121–36 in *Margins of Writing, Origins of Cultures*. Edited by S. Sanders. Chicago: The Oriental Institute of the University of Chicago.
2008   "Writing and Identity." Pages 117–22 in *Anatolian Interfaces: Hittites, Greeks, and Their Neighbors. Proceedings of an International Conference on Cross-Cultural Interaction, September 17–19, 2004, Emory University, Atlanta, GA*. Edited by B. J. Collins, M. Bachvarova, and I. Rutherford. Oxford: Oxbow.
2010   *Hieroglyphic Luwian. An Introduction with Original Texts*. 2nd rev. ed. Wiesbaden: Harrassowitz.
forthcoming   *Schrift und Schriftlichkeit. Die anatolische Hieroglyphenschrift*.

Rieken, E.
2004   "Luwisch tarza/i-." Pages 457–68 in *Per Aspera ad astericos. studia indogermanica in honorem Jens Elmegšrd Rasmussen sexagenarii idibus Martiis anno MMIV*. Edited by A. Hyllested, et al. IBS 112. Innsbruck: Innsbruck: Institut für Sprachen und Literaturen der Universität Innsbruck.

Rieken, E. and Yakubovich, I.
2010   "The New Values of Luwian Signs L 319 And L 175." Pages 199–219 in *ipamati kistamati pari tumatimis, Luwian and Hittite Studies presented to J. David Hawkins on the Occasion of His 70th Birthday*. Edited by I. Singer. Emery and ClaireYass Publications in Archaeology, Institute of Archaeology, Tel Aviv University, Tel Aviv.

Simon, Z.
forthcoming "Where is the Land of Sura of the Hieroglyphic Luwian Inscription KARKAMIŠ A4b and Why Were Cappadocians Called Syrians by Greeks?" *AoF*.
Singer, I.
2006 "The Hittites and the Bible Revisited." Pages 723–56 in *I Will Speak the Riddles of Ancient Times" : Archaeological and Historical Studies in Honor of Amihai Mazar on the Occasion of His Sixtieth Birthday*. Edited by A. M. Maeir and P. de Miroschedji; Winona Lake, Ind.: Eisenbrauns.
Starke, F.
1997 "Sprachen und Schriften in Karkamis." Pages 381–95 in *Ana šadî Labnāni lū allik. Beiträge zu altorientalischen und mittelmeerischen Kulturen. Festschrift für Wolfgang Röllig*. AOAT 247. Edited by B. Pongratz-Leisten, H. Kühne and P. Xella, Neukirchen-Vluyn: Neukirchener Verlag.
Tadmor, H.
1961 "Que and Muṣri." *IEJ* 11: 143–50.
Tekoğlu, R., and A. Lemaire
2000 "La bilingue royale louvito-phénicienne de Çineköy." *Académie des inscriptions et belles-lettres, comptes rendus*, 2000: 961–1006.
Tischler, J.
2001 *Hethitisches Handwörterbuch. Mit dem Wortschatz der Nachbarsprachen*. IBS 102. Innsbruck: Institut für Sprachen und Literaturen der Universität Innsbruck.
Wright, W.
1886 *The Empire of the Hittites*. London.
Yakubovich, I.
2002 "Nugae Luvicae." Pages 189–209 in *Anatolian Languages*. Edited by Vitaly Shevoroshkin and Paul J. Sidwell. Canberra: Association for the History of Language.
2008 "Hittite-Luvian Bilingualism and the Origin of Anatolian Hieroglyphs." Pages 9–36 in *Acta Linguistica Petropolitana*. Edited by N. N. Kazansky, Transactions of the Institute for Linguistic Studies, IV/1. St. Petersburg: Nauka.
2010a *Sociolinguistics of the Luvian Language*. Studies in Indo-European Languages and Linguistics 2. Leiden: Brill.
2010b "The West Semitic God El in Anatolin Hieroglyphic Transmission." Pages 385–98 in *Pax Hethitica. Studies on the Hittites and Their Neighbours in Honour of Itamar Singer*. Edited by Y. Cohen, A. Gilan and J. L. Miller. Wiesbaden: Harrassowitz.
forthcoming "The Reading of the Anatolian Hieroglyph *216 (*ARHA*)." Proceedings of the Eighth International Congress of Hittitology, Warsaw 2011.
Younger, K. Lawson
1998 "The Phoenician Inscription of Azatiwada. An Integrated Reading." *JSS* 43:11–47.

www.ingramcontent.com/pod-product-compliance
Lightning Source LLC
Chambersburg PA
CBHW022106160426
43198CB00008B/371